CONTENTS

1 INTRODUCTION
2 ASPECTS OF STRATEGY
3 COMMUNICATION AND ITS PROBLEMS
4 ANALYSING RATHER THAN DESCRIBING
5 STRATEGY'S ROLE WHEN PLANNING IN A BUSINESS SETTING
6 THE DECISION MAKING PROCESS
7 INTERPRETATION AND ERRORS
8 WHAT IS STRATEGY? WHAT ARE TACTICS?
9 THE IMPORTANCE OF THE ENTRY DATA
10 STRATEGY AS A PROCESS
11 THE MARKETING STRATEGY SYNTHETIC MODEL
11.1 STRATEGIC DRIFT
11.2 INNOVATION AND DIFFERENTIATION
11.3 DESIGN OF THE OFFERING
11.4 THE BUSINESS MODEL
11.5 SEGMENTATION AND TARGETING
11.6 PRACTICAL EXAMPLE
11.7 WHAT IS SWOT USED FOR?
11.8 COMPETITIVE ADVANTAGE
11.9 POSITIONING
11.10 STRATEGIC COMMUNICATION

11.11 RECAPITULATION

11.12 PRICE AND DIFFERENTIATION

12 TACTICS. REINFORCING DIFFERENTIATION

13 THE SALES PROCESS

14 LEADERSHIP AND CHANGE

15 EPILOGUE

16 ABOUT THE AUTHOR

> Communicate effectively with your team by sharing an agile model of strategy

MARKETING STRATEGY

Can you tell me yours?

A small & medium company approach

Hugo Rubio

Author: Hugo Rubio
Translated by Julia Rubio and Becky Tate

Registered as Intellectual Property 01/2016/603
Copyright © 2016 by Hugo Rubio Vega
All rights reserved.

First edition, June 2016
Second edition, April 2020

To my friends, who share their lives with me, because that is what life is all about.

1 INTRODUCTION

In the business world we constantly use concepts that have poorly defined content and vague practical application. One of these concepts is that of strategy.

Everyone talks about strategy and clearly a strategy, which is defined, understood and subject to continuous improvement, is needed. However, if I were to ask you what your business strategy was, that would probably cause some problem. If I went on to ask you to write it down, the problem would grow bigger. Following that, if I asked you what your competitive advantage was, you would possibly give me the same answer, when in actual fact you would simply be referring to one of your strengths. If I then inquired about your tactics, you may well become quite unnerved.

This book is not about creating academic definitions. It is aimed at creating a language strong enough to move from concept to action in order to build an organized and monitored marketing plan. Perhaps most importantly, this language can then be shared throughout the length and breadth of the business team. In this way, when a strategic problem is referred to, we will know specifically what is being talked about and identify it with precision. Internal team communication will improve alongside our analysis capacity and we will hence be able to advance quickly to a resolution.

The aim is to establish a useful and simple model that can define the implementation of a strategic marketing process within a business plan. The components of the strategic process should be nurtured and the results mark the difference between success and failure.

And then you, as a strategist, will have to put it into practice.

2 ASPECTS OF STRATEGY

Firstly, we should clarify that there are numerous types of strategy. We will not be providing definitions, although I do recognize that a strong definition can be really inspiring. We could talk about manufacturing strategy, for example, to address the issues related to this field. We could refer to financial or corporate strategies or strategies for mergers and acquisitions; organizational or human resource strategy amongst others could also be featured.

This book however, will focus and expand on the concept of strategic marketing. Nevertheless, as a director, manager or salesperson of any business, it is vital that you identify all your own particular business strategies and satisfy all of the different requirements. Strategic marketing is possibly one of the least identified strategies.

'Stratego' was the name given to Greek generals. An army's victory or defeat was dependant on the general's decision making when assigning and positioning resources on the battlefield. In the same way, a director's decision in the business world, regarding its resources and market positioning can lead to success or failure.

Perhaps you have heard on the news that a certain country has launched tactical missiles close to a certain border, or that another has installed a base of strategic missiles; you might ask yourself what is the difference between the two? Tactical missiles are inexpensive and can be transported quickly and economically to where they are needed. That is why they are called tactical. Strategic missiles, on the other hand, are very big, expensive to design and build; once installed they must be able to reach their target. If they are badly designed it will take years to fix and you will be unprotected whilst dedicating more time and money to resolving the issue. That is why they are called strategic.

The concept of strategy is associated with four fundamental aspects, which are **decisions, investment, time and opportunity cost**. Decisions are taken continuously at several levels, not only at a business level but also at a domestic and personal level. We all know that there are some decisions that are easy to make, although others are much more difficult. This is due to the fact that this latter type of decision incorporates the second and third aspect, those of investment and time limits which affect decision making. A decision is strategic when it involves large resources and imposes time conditions in the future.

The fourth aspect is that of opportunity cost. Logically, these decisions are made to meet a certain objective. If we make a mistake, we will have lost the opportunity to drive the situation due to dependence on resources and time. It is interesting to observe that it is not always necessary for our current project to fail in order to incur high opportunity costs. We simply lose what we would have gained had we invested in a better project. That is why these strategic decisions are difficult to make.

The opportunity cost is the cost of the opportunity that we have not chosen. Put in a different way, it is what we don't gain by not making the choice. This gain can be higher or lower than what we obtain with the option that we have chosen. For example, if you are a professional person who earns 100 euros for every hour worked and you take 3 hours off to run a personal errand, the opportunity cost for that errand is very high, maybe even higher than hiring someone to run the errand for you. This example is obvious, but when translated into a business setting, it becomes less obvious. Lots of businesses have operations with very high opportunity costs, and due to this, they stop performing tasks that are much more important or productive.

A typical example would be when businesses provide certain

components internally instead of buying them from the outside market. If there is nothing more productive to be done, resources can be provided internally. The less productive you are, the more sense it makes to do this, although you are probably also being less competitive internally than you would be with the outside market, which creates a vicious circle of strategic drift.

For example, if I am unemployed, it makes sense for me to bake my own bread at home and to also do the housework. I will never be as efficient as the baker or a professional cleaner, but I will save money. On the other hand, if I work, I wouldn't change my working hours to bake bread or clean my house because I would lose money. The justification that it is cheaper to provide services internally does not make sense if you do not compare it to the income that you are missing out on and with the opportunity that you are missing. Providing for oneself internally can be a symptom or recognition of a lack of competitiveness in one's own industry.

We need to be constantly identifying and defining what is strategically the most important for our business and focus on this without distractions. Remember to measure your opportunity cost, evaluate the effect it has on resources in terms of time and money and make the appropriate decision. These are the components of strategic decisions.

3 COMMUNICATION AND ITS PROBLEMS

Internal communication is fundamental to execute any project. Many projects fail because of lack of good communication. This applies not only to business projects but also to families, sports, social events and even between politicians and citizens.

Communication is referred to throughout this book, both external communication with clients and internal communication with a focus on the business, its employees and its management team. This book aims to focus on communication within a management team and for this reason, a strategic model is introduced for reference. The idea is that if a team can use a model and refer to it, the abstract concepts can be visualized and used in a practical and systematic way.

I am aware that this is not simple. Over the years, I have been able to observe constantly that the ideas that we have determine the way we think and communicate. Recently, one of my friends who frequently travels by car for professional and personal reasons, mentioned that he went to the garage, to change his tyres for winter ones. The conversation went something like this:

- "I would like to put winter tyres on my car, but I have been told that the car will run differently and I wanted to know if this is true."

- "No, cars run fine, they make a little bit more noise and the maximum speed is lower, but they run well."

- "So you are sure that the car will run the same?"

- "Yes, exactly the same."

So my friend decides to have the tyres changed. After a while, he goes back to collect his car. He drives his car around the block before returning to the garage to complain that something has not been fitted properly- "There must be a loose screw, a broken bolt or something, because the car swerves when going over 50 kilometres per hour only." The mechanic proceeds to look into the issue.

- "No, nothing is wrong, it is all fine."

- "But the car keeps swerving"

- "Oh! That's because of the winter tyres."

- "But, I asked you twice if the car would continue to run the same way!"

- "Yes, it runs the same way but the tyres do have that effect."

My friend was surprised. How on earth was it possible that there was a misunderstanding regarding such a specific situation?

I will continue to explain something that happened to me recently as well whilst away on holiday. I was going from the north of Burgos, along the GR99, the (the natural course of the river Ebro) towards the Mediterranean. As I was nearing Soria night was falling. I stopped at a petrol station where they told me that in Soria, on the road to Madrid, I could find a campsite. On arrival I asked a passerby:

- "Please, could you let me know where the campsite is?"

-"There isn't a campsite in Soria."

- "But, I have just been told that there is a campsite on the road to Madrid!"

-"That's right, just 3 kilometres down that road."

Apparently, that campsite 3 kilometres outside of Soria was not considered by the passerby to be in Soria. Had I not insisted, I would not have found it.

When I travel and I have to ask for directions, I do this several times. I ask the same questions twice to different passersby. Sometimes they give me different replies, or additional comments or details that are extremely useful. For example, if you ask how to reach a certain destination, they could point you in the right direction. If you ask the question in a slightly different way, they could tell you what the road is like or will even advise on an alternate route. If you ask one passerby, they may say that you will arrive in an hour, if you ask another, they will say it's 15 kilometres away. Sometimes, you even have to mention that you are cycling to your destination. Even if you are on a bike when you ask and you assume that they are aware of how you will be getting there, people do not always realize. It is interesting how people communicate.

If communicating simple information can be problematic, then communicating complex information can be even more difficult. This book aims to facilitate, the communication of information when designing a business strategy, with the goal of communicating as systematically, productively and efficiently as possible.

4 ANALYSING RATHER THAN DESCRIBING

When we talk about marketing, most people tend to think of one thing: they associate it with advertising. However, marketing is a discipline that is rather more complicated and contains a very solid planning process. One of its layers is strategy and this is the one that we will be focusing our attention on.

Reality demonstrates that small companies frequently lack organised marketing plans with no marketing department. When resources and time are scarce there always tends to be something more urgent to prioritize over effective planning.

Furthermore, there is still an additional block to the creation of a marketing plan, which is the creation of a purely descriptive plan with the mindset: If we already know what we are going to write in the plan, why should we waste our time creating it? Simply transferring it to paper will not have much value.

This is usually the thought process. The result is the lack of planning. However, creating a plan does make a lot of sense. Issues tend to appear when asked to explain a plan verbally. It is commonly said that one only truly understands something when you are able to explain it. If on top of that more doubts emerge when asked to write it down, further reflection is required. When something is written down, the quality and coherence of your ideas improve. This is called **epistemic writing**. The planning process is what really matters. Let us remember that famous phrase from Dwight D. Eisenhower, *'Plans are worthless, but planning is everything.'*

The real value of planning appears when the focus shifts **from**

being descriptive to being analytical. The designing of a marketing plan should always be analytical; the process of preparing it and the control involved should be the motor for generating ideas in the business. This is the only way to establish an innovative process in our company.

So, what are the characteristics of analytical pieces of work? The analytical process tends to identify the problems (not the symptoms), and then find the common roots and the causes. These pieces of work then propose several solutions which are evaluated both individually and collectively and explain the benefits of the chosen solution. To apply this to our particular case, we would need to use a methodological structure for reference and knowledge at a business level and in addition, a reference point which is particular to the case.

This methodology can be applied to any type of situation - academic, personal or professional. It can also be used in forms, reports, essays, process improvement cases, sales or general transfer of information. Over the years, I have often seen cases where I have asked professionals for a written update on a situation or issue, which they have found very difficult to produce no matter how brief. I will continue to explain the different phases of the analytical methodology in a simple and clear way:

Structure of an analytical study:
1. Introduction: Description of the problem and its surroundings
2. Identification of the problem: Relation of the effects and the identification of its possible causes in a justified way (its causes, not just the commonalities.) Use of analytical tools.
3. Identifying solutions: Relation of the possible solutions. Evaluating each one in a justified way.
4. Selection of the solutions: Identifying criteria for the

selection of the solution or collective solutions, indicating the advantages and disadvantages in a justified way.
5. Conclusion: Justifying the chosen solution. Explaining how it can solve the problem.

Additionally, we need to conduct this analysis within a structured and methodological process, using content which specifically relates to the material or problem in hand and applying it to the context of the issue: Structure, content and context.

In this way we have the problem and its environment defined, as follows:

1. Structure (analytics, form, thesis, project, plan, etc.)
2. Content (knowledge upon which we build)
3. Context (actual reference point from where we work from, industry, market, problem, etc.)

Following this simple methodology allows for more flexibility in the creation any kind of document and improves the quality of its content.

5 STRATEGY'S ROLE WHEN PLANNING IN A BUSINESS SETTING

In the previous chapter I mentioned that, in addition to the analytical process outlined, it is also important to develop a structured framework, content and context.

In a business setting, depending on its size and environment, different types of plans can be found -corporate plans, departmental plans, negotiation plans, amongst others. In this book we will refer to the planning of marketing, which at the same time can be executed at a corporate level, departmentally or within a process of negotiation. Diverse plans and their aims and objectives should be aligned in every way. Not only do marketing plans within a department or corporation need to be aligned, but financial and manufacturing plans should be too.

The structural framework which we will follow is called SOSTAC®, designed by Paul Smith (prsmith.org) and explained in his book "The SOSTAC® Guide to Your Perfect Digital Marketing Plan".

SOSTAC®is an acronym which derives from the different phases of marketing planning. These analytical phases are: Situation analysis, Objectives, Strategy, Tactics, Action and Control. This is a great book to guide the structure of marketing planning. The framework is simple and easy for immediate application. I would recommend using this as a reference point when planning and to locate your marketing strategy within that plan.

As previously mentioned, we sometimes identify marketing with advertising. In reality, advertising is one of the approximately fifteen tools of communication that falls under one of the famous '7 Ps of Marketing', the P of Promotion (communication). All of the Ps together form the 'Tactical' part of the marketing plan. However, the strategic phase comes before all of this. As a result we can talk about tactical marketing if what we are analysing is tactics or strategic marketing with a focus on strategy.

Reality shows us that businesses tend to ignore strategy and tend to focus on tactics or on direct implementation. Day to day urgency makes us focus on tactics and action. We often put into action communication programmes, promotional campaigns, web pages or commercialized products or services without having previously undertaken adequate study or evaluation.

We do this because we are in a rush, because we don't know exactly how to execute this strategic analysis and because it is easier to focus directly on the action. Tactical strategy is much easier to focus on. However, avoiding the strategic phase at the onset means we end up rejecting or postponing decisions later due to the difficulties created through missing out this important step.

Look at how business meetings tend to be run, in so many cases. Usually, meetings start out by stating the problem, immediately followed by group members contributing their individual ideas for solutions. Any reference to the word strategy is usually vague and imprecise and is very rarely defined. These discussions tend to cause multiple ideas which are dispersed and have no correlation with one another. After a while, when everyone is tired and unable to reach a consensus, someone will pipe up "Okay, so let's do something, let's focus on the action." Does this sound familiar?

Once again, the focus is on the action before really defining the strategy -this is an error.

Solving this problem is not easy, but that is the aim of this book.

6 THE DECISION MAKING PROCESS

There are many situations where decision making is required within business related activities. Decisions should be taken using a methodical process.

Usually, we rely on data, which is the easiest accessible tool. As Sherlock Holmes once pointed out to Watson, *'It is a capital mistake to theorize before one has data'*.

We can generate information by using that data. For example, going from a set of numerical data and analysing it with a linear regression tool permits us to discover the type of correlation that exists. We have moved from data to information.

This is not an automatic step. When moving from data to information there is always a process of interpretation and due of this, there is always room for error. We will go on to talk about this later.

Once we have the information we can then convert this to knowledge. For this we need experience in a determined sector, industry or discipline. This also requires that information is kept up to date and enriched incrementally. Here too the possibility exists of committing errors, precisely based on the fact of the experience we have accumulated and the constraints that it generates.

There are authors that propose a further step, which would be application of wisdom, which is a term that I will not attempt to define.

All of this is done with the aim of making a decision in relation to the opportunity cost and to create an action. We can see these steps in the following graphic:

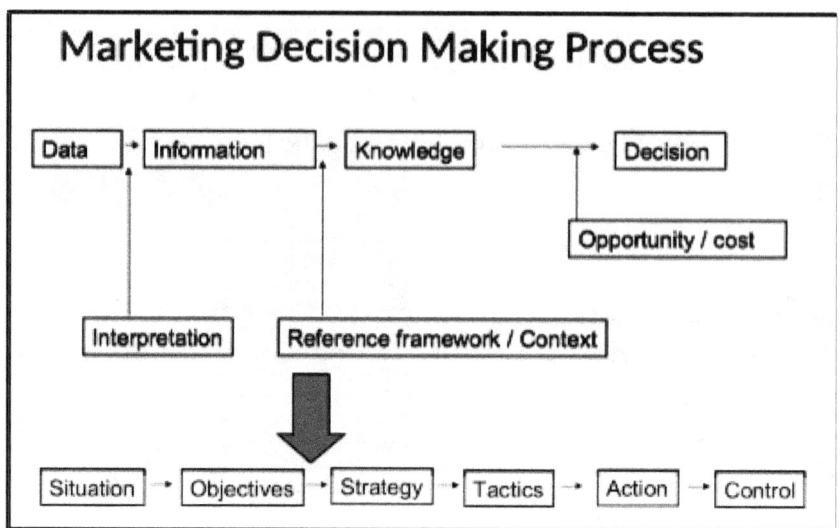

We are able to observe that decisions can be made in the situational analysis, for example, deciding how and in how much depth the environment is analysed, in the objectives definition, review and elimination steps, in the strategic analysis, the tactical stage and also in the action and control steps.

All these phases have their importance, but we will focus specifically on just one of them, the strategic phase.

It's true that some people have the capacity to sense what is happening around them and even when improvising they do very well. However, this does not mean to say that this process does not exist, even if it is produced in an unconscious manner. You could say that intuition is an advanced capacity of being able to process data and converting it into knowledge.

For example, you could ask a shepherd for tomorrow's weather forecast. The shepherd would respond with his prognosis and you could ask him how he knows the answer. The shepherd may not want to explain this to you. He has the knowledge but may not know how to explain it. In an unconscious way, he has seen the clouds, the direction of the wind, the variation of the temperature, the behaviour of different animals and other natural factors. He has gathered data and has processed this with methodology acquired over the course of the years. That capacity for gathering information and processing it in an unconscious manner is intuition (**tacit knowledge**, a concept introduced by the scientist and philosopher Michael Polanyi. This is knowledge that has been acquired in a practical way, difficult to articulate and explain).

On the other hand, playing the lottery because you have a hunch is not intuition, in real terms it is nothing at all.

The same can be said about improvising. Improvising is almost always referred to when the result is positive, for example "We had to improvise and we got out of that mess." Sometimes it is done in a negative sense such as "We can't spend the entire day improvising." However, in general, when we talk about 'the great capacity of improvising' is because the results are satisfactory.

It is an important observation that when you improvise and it goes well, it is because you are well prepared. When you listen to Jimmy Hendrix improvising he is able to do so because he knows his craft so well. When a fire-fighter faces an emergency and he needs to improvise a solution, this is generally based on training and preparation. Realistically, if someone does not know how to play the guitar and starts playing a few chords no one would say, "Look how he's improvising!" Improvising is also based on knowledge but the planning process is never exempt.

Intuition and improvisation are ultimately ways of handling data and converting this into information, using a mental process based on tacit knowledge built on experience and done in an unconscious manner. Could this be defined as wisdom?

There are people that have a special ability; able to use intuition or accumulate wisdom. They are the fortunate visionaries able to observe events and make the right decisions. For the rest of us who are not capable of this, well we will continue with methodology and planning!

7 INTERPRETATION AND ERRORS

We mentioned in the last chapter how going from data to information and to knowledge may lead us to commit errors of interpretation. These errors can be classified in a generic way such as **errors of type 1, 2, or 3, the Cognitive Dissonance and the Criteria of the Own Reference**. By avoiding them we can improve the analytical process, differentiating causes from effects, identifying problems and proposing solutions.

Identifying the real causes of events is complicated. In the first place, we must recognize that we are hardly ever going to find the true cause. The cause, as such, does not exist. It depends on the **evaluation criteria**. This may seem strange to you, but this it is what keeps thought processes flowing. "Thou shalt not kill except when..." and a long list of exceptions begins. It is a different scenario and people will say, we are no longer talking about the same thing.

Many intercultural problems are generated by ignoring this principle. What can be a virtue for me can be a mortal sin for another. What is the truth? **As the philosopher Hilary Putnam affirms, the truth depends on the values of each person, each culture**. This is called pluralism (not to be confused with relativism). Pluralism is to admit that there is a plurality of criteria and that all with value that should be recognized. Relativism, on the other hand, tends to detract from different criteria on the premise that "anything goes".

So, if you are ever told not to make a value judgement, you could respond without fear of being wrong, that you are not judging but simply making an evaluation. This is something you have the right to do and that is necessary to understand an event and create an opinion.

Some types of interpretation errors can be attributed to the Criteria of the Own Reference, which explains how experience influences us when making decisions. These are inevitably based on a modelling and assessment of possible future scenarios. As human beings, we tend to base ourselves on our own experiences, on what has happened to us in our case. In the case of others, this will always seem alien to us.

It cannot be any other way. We will always be slaves to what has happened to us and we will tend to generalise our particular experience. In this life, experience is always individual, although the most valuable thing is general experience which is the result of many individual experiences. Many people, for example, after a stock market disappointment do not invest in the stock market again. They make their individual case a general one.

You have to be very careful with this. We cannot get rid of it but at least we have to know that it exists, that it restricts us and that we have to consider the way in which it is affects us. Learning from others' experience by reading and listening is the only alternative; nevertheless, everything always needs to go through our own experiential filter. Reason will struggle against the heart on many occasions.

I remember when I built my house. At that time, ten people who did not know each other, defying all kinds of odds, embarked on the adventure. We assumed some calculated risks: "It will be the first housing cooperative I have seen that goes well" said the lawyer when we formed the community of owners. That later paid off. While we were building, older members of the family insisted that I install cast iron radiators. They are the best, they said, they give more heat over more time.

Being an engineer, I asked for their rationale. I did not understand how it would produce more heat as this was surely conditioned by the boiler and the thermostat. There was no way to reason with them. They believed that the current aluminium radiators were bad and the cast iron ones were good. 'Pay attention to us!' they told me.

I gave this topic a lot of thought, until I eventually understood it. In the "old days", boilers burned wood or charcoal. These boilers have a feature that restricts them from being automatically regulated, that is, they depend on a person who physically carries and literally throws the fuel into the boiler. Pieces of wood or coal shovels had to be handled.

A direct consequence of this characteristic is that throughout the night, the boiler remains unattended since there is no one to replace the fuel. So, to maintain the temperature of the room all night, it is very important that the radiator has good thermal inertia, meaning that it stores a lot of heat; this is achieved through having a greater mass. The cast iron radiator stores heat and releases it throughout the night.
Obviously, this is not necessary when using liquid or gaseous fuels, or even wood in the form of pellets, which allow automatic feeding of the boiler, regulated by a thermostat. In this case, radiators of low thermal inertia are even better as they heat up fast.

But all this just didn't matter and there was no way of reasoning with them. Cast iron radiators had always been the best and everyone knew that.

This would be nothing more than a funny anecdote, if it were not for the fact that decisions are made following very similar processes. Our own experience conditions us, and too often prevents us from identifying the real causes of the events. Just like a small child would often do, always ask yourself, "why?"

We can make mistakes when trying to relate causes and their effects. The first is the so-called Type 1 error. This error occurs when we attribute an effect to a cause, and this is not the case. For example, we perform a rain dance and it rains. From here we conclude that there is a relationship and every time we need it to rain, we do the dance. You may think that this example is too childish, but replace the rain dance with taking the saint out to a procession in times of drought and you will see that the concept is very similar. The strength of one's own experience is great, and has been used collectively for millennia.

The second type of error, the Type 2 error, is the opposite. It occurs when there is a connected relationship that has not been identified. For example, I could think that not washing my hands before eating does not affect whether or not I become ill. It may be that we have not yet discovered the relationship but it is worse to simply dismiss it. For example, I can fool myself and think that smoking does not do anything to me. Or that driving fast does not increase the possibility of having an accident.

Those responsible for managing the road network know this very well. Each time the maximum speed is increased by a percentage on a certain bend in the road, the percentage of deaths per year increases. This is a direct relation. Nevertheless, on a personal level, we reject it. We cheat ourselves in a process called cognitive dissonance. We are aware that there is a dissonance of knowledge and generate arguments of defence, even if we deceive ourselves.

It is curious to see how the criteria of the reference itself work here. One way or another, we are aware that driving faster increases the chances of an accident but we reject the idea, partly because on a personal level we have not had any accidents. When you have had one, you behave differently. Since most living people have never died (although some maintain that they have), we do not have the experience of dying and we literally defy death. As soon as a point system is established for the driving licence and we are fined severely, the loss ratio is surprisingly reduced. It is that experience of being fined and punished, that we then react to. Curiously, we fear being fined more than death. These represent Type 2 errors.

The most dangerous of all, in my opinion, is the Type 3 error. This error misinterprets the question and generates a correct answer to the wrong question. It is usually difficult to identify because the wide breadth of the response can make us forget the cause we are looking for. An example of this would be confusing tactics with strategy. It is typical for example, to see marketing plans with a detailed implementation plan about an unidentified strategy or tactical communication plans (media plan) without any elaboration of the correct communication content.

In my opinion and as an example, wanting to energise the labour market by changing types of contracts is a Type 3 error. This is not the cause of unemployment. These kinds of contracts can tactically affect recruitment, but not strategically. The only way to improve the labour market is by improving competitiveness and education.

I do not ask my university students any questions in their exams. They have to identify them, extracting them from the case material. If they are incorrect in the identification of the question, in the diagnosis of the problem making a Type 3 error, they fail. At the end of the day, as some Eastern cultures say, the answer lies in the question. If I define the question, I am already telling them the answer they have to write. I already assume that they know how to do that!

We all look for answers, but the secret is that the answer depends on the question. If the question is wrong, the answer will have no value. In my PhD program, the first course I attended was "How to identify questions for research". First you have to ask the questions around the problem. If the questions are good, the research will make sense and generate answers. Otherwise, one can easily fall into a false discourse, devoid of content, such as, for example, astrology.

In the real world there are no established questions, we have to identify them ourselves at a personal, social and economic level. If we identify them poorly and dedicate our effort and resources to the wrong problem, we will fail.

8 WHAT IS STRATEGY? WHAT ARE TACTICS?

There is a great inhibitor to the realisation of the strategic plan and this is the ease and immediacy of a tactical plan, particularly in the area of communication. Carrying out a communication or sales plan is something that everyone understands and sees as necessary. In addition, it is usually urgent. Due to this, day-to-day dynamics tend to lead us in this direction. Once we start developing the tactical and action phases, we tend to stop paying attention to the strategic phase.

That is why it is very important to separate these two phases and understand that before developing the tactics, you have to develop the strategy and verify that it is correct, auditing the competitive advantage of the company. If there is no competitive advantage, you have to create it through strategy. If it exists, it will need to be continuously improved.

The sequence is as follows, following the SOSTAC® planning structure:

1. Situational Analysis
2. Establishment of Objectives
3. Audit of the Competitive Advantage: do we have it or not?
4. Strategic Analysis: Improvement or generation of strategies
5. Audit of competitive advantage (review after improvement, do we have an advantage now?)
6. Tactical Analysis. Development of the 7 Ps
7. Action
8. Control

The plan can be divided into two parts: the first, SOS, ends with the definition of the strategy, and the second, TAC, begins with the tactics. The strategy, which we will develop later, incorporates the design of our proposals for the chosen clients. Tactics implement this design in a detailed way because implementing a non-existent design does not make sense. Strategy is necessary before tactics. Tactics are made up of the well known **7Ps of marketing, Product, Price, Place (channel), Promotions (communication), People, Processes, and Physical Evidence**.

The development of tactics is therefore simpler and more familiar to us. Throughout this book we will try to develop strategy in more detail since it entails greater difficulty.

Both tactics and strategy will contribute to the improvement of our business. When we perform the GAP analysis, this analysis allows us to identify what we lack (the gap) to achieve our objectives. We need to take into account that we must have identified activities of both types. If, for example, we find only tactical actions, we will notice immediately that something is wrong with our business plan since we also have to identify strategic actions.

GAP Analisis and Planning

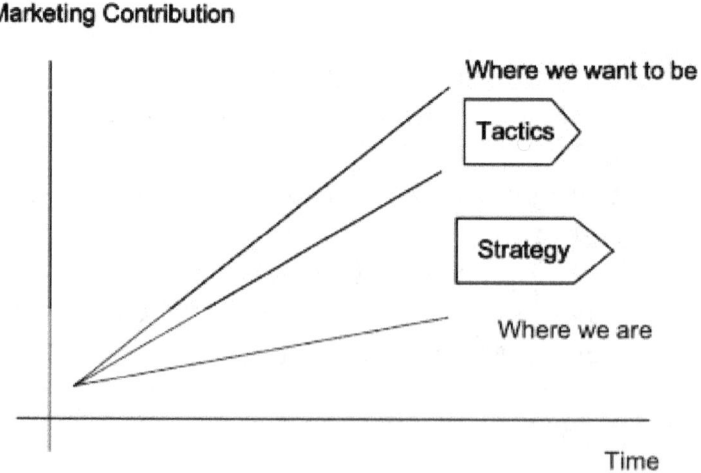

But remember that you must not develop tactics (the 7 Ps) without having designed the strategy before. Tactics are based on the development of the 7 Ps and the strategy, we propose, in the components that make up the Synthetic Model of Marketing Strategy MSSM®.

9 THE IMPORTANCE OF THE ENTRY DATA

We have seen how the SOSTAC® model begins with a study of the situation. This study is fundamental and unfortunately little is done in practice. This manual does not pretend to explain how to do it although we will at least identify the main parts so that the reader can later go further into detail where necessary.

It is interesting to note that many companies are beginning to contract or implement data analysis services internally. Moving from data to information is not easy, it requires methodologies and tools; it is fundamental to have the entry data.

Companies often have data, at least their own, in production databases. The production databases are those used by the company's operational systems. For example, the warehouse application normally only has data relating to warehouses and is updated with the actual activity of the warehouse. It may not contain historical data or relationships with other areas of the company. The same could be said of other applications such as accounting, sales or billing, for example. There are applications, known as Enterprise Resource Planning or ERPs that integrate many of these applications into one, maintaining a unique image of the data. Even so, it is necessary to create new informational databases and differentiate them from operational ones, in order to be able to exploit the data and turn it into information. All this is a big project in itself.

Informational databases must therefore be kept updated, clear of redundant and inappropriately structured data. In turn, we must have several historical copies in order to extract information on trends and developments. Working on them will in turn produce information and knowledge.

In addition to the internal data, there is external data. Knowing about the industry data referenced to industries, markets, products, customers and competitors is fundamental, at least up to a certain level. This can be done by obtaining primary data directly from the environment, or by acquiring secondary data, previously collected by another entity. The second option will usually be cheaper and faster.

Normally a company will know the environment in which it moves quite well, although trusting that this is always true is a great source of errors. Some companies hire services for other consulting firms to provide them with industry and market data and even advise them on their own operations. This is a typical example of strategic consulting. It is necessary to anticipate the future in some way. An illustrative example we have is the fashion industry. Knowing trends and getting what is going to be in vogue for next season is essential, since you have to stock up in the summer for the autumn campaign. Committing an error here would be ruinous.

Many modern operating environments, especially those focused on online businesses, already have their own subsystem of data analysis, often in the client-related application, usually called CRM (customer relationship management). Some companies create a competitive advantage based on these tools. For example, a fashion company may know immediately what is being sold, without waiting for the end of the season to analyse the data. Knowing what is being sold in real time can allow you to manage warehouses more efficiently, modify the production chain to provide the market with what you want in the specific geographical location and also modify prices dynamically. This in turn strengthens the company's positioning, improves the brand image, and increases customer loyalty.

You may have heard about new concepts related to data, such as Open Data and Big Data. Open data refers to the publication of data that is normally in the hands of the government, so that it can be exploited by the public to create new services. Big Data refers to huge amounts of data whose exploitation is difficult and for which special techniques, capable of managing large volumes, are needed.

Therefore, the situational analysis aims to obtain data and then information about the environment. The environment can be modelled in a simple way as explained below.

In the first place, there is the market in which the company competes, constituted by the Company itself, the Clients and the Competitors. This is called analysis of the three C's, or the competitive market.

A market is not an industry, although sometimes the two concepts can coincide. The next level of analysis will be that of the industry; in which industry we compete and how this conditions us. This environment is known as the microenvironment.

The third scenario is the macro-environment and it is the political, social, legal and economic environment in which we work. This environment, unlike the other two, is unable to be modified by the company. We have to keep an eye on it to accommodate and anticipate its changes when needed.

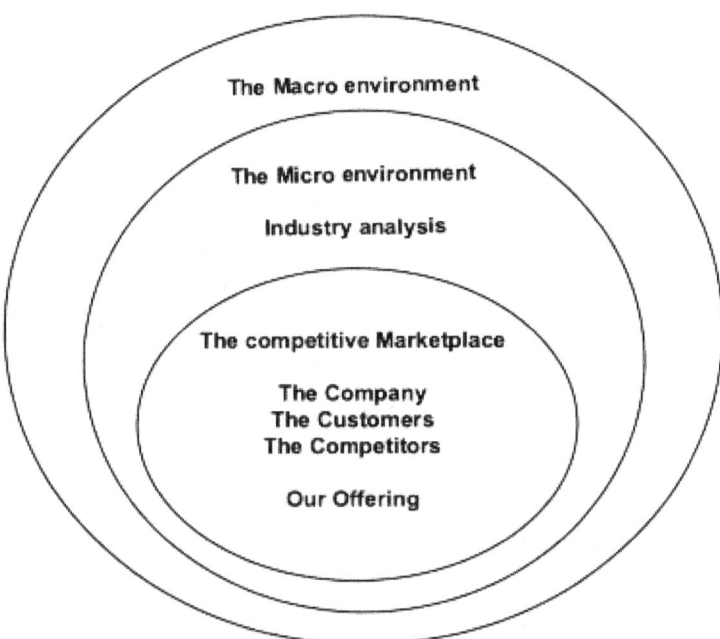

There are many tools and models to perform situational analysis. It is not the purpose of this book to propose tools for analysing the environment, but since what interests us is the strategic point of view, we will choose a few examples in order to reach this understanding.

The simplest way for us will always be to start with our own company, since our company data will be the most accessible. However, although the data is within our reach it is not always easy to access and turn into information.

The first step will be to classify our sales by products or groups of products according to their competitive position in the market. By competitive position we mean the position they occupy in relation to competitors and the corresponding market according to their growth potential. This is usually enough to make a start. In fact, when business managers are asked questions such as: "How much does a certain market grow?" "What market share does your product have?" "How much does a certain segment contribute to the benefit of the company?" the answers are usually along the lines of: "I don't know, although we have the data somewhere"

To begin with, we can rely on the tools known as the Boston Matrix and the Directional Matrix (also called the General Electric matrix). They are widely known. You can find information about them from various sources. We will use them later when we develop the concept of offering. The relevant concept of these tools is in the idea of market growth. We will always go to the markets that grow, we will measure results against these markets and we will develop capacities for these markets. This is the reason for situational analysis. Always keep in mind that the main result of this analysis is the identification of growing markets and the company's adaptation to them.

Using these tools requires us to know what our competitors do. To a certain extent, it is necessary to monitor what products they offer and in what markets they are located. Also, obviously, we must know our customers, as we will see later in detail. All this cannot be done at once; it must be done incrementally by converting data into information at each stage.

In addition to these tools, we can include the Ansoff matrix. This matrix is very simple; its use involves making decisions about the allocation of the company's resources. Remember that describing scenarios is very simple, but making decisions that involve allocations of expensive and long-term resources is not. The Ansoff matrix requires you to set priorities to devote resources to some of the four quadrants that you consider to be the possible strategic options. The company has scarce resources and therefore will have to choose to develop in some of the options proposed by Ansoff, but it will be difficult to focus on all.

Doing a bit of everything is a romantic idea but it takes a lot of focus and many resources to succeed. I usually argue that we have three basic resources: time, energy and focus (I develop these aspects in my other book, **Economy to Leave Home**). The Ansoff matrix helps us decide where to put these three resources, which will additionally require funding.

ANSOFF's Matrix	Traditional PRODUCT New	
Traditional **MARKET**	**Penetration:** Dedicating resources to increase our market share	**Product Development:** Dedicating resources to product development, new or through diversification (horizontally and vertically)
New	**Market Development:** Dedicating resource to develop a new market in other geographies or in new segments	**Diversification:** Dedicating resources to develop new products in new markets through the development of conglomerates, acquisitions or the genuine development of new products/markets such as digital music

Above the market in which we compete is the industry in which we compete, or the micro-environment. The concept 'industry' is complex, requires knowledge and years of working experience to understand it. The example of the seed industry is an eye-opening one. It is one of the oldest in human history and of which people have limited knowledge due to the complex technology required for the genetic manipulation on which it is based. A few companies, with very advanced technology, dominate this market, one that has undergone a profound transformation and which is posing many ethical conflicts.

To study the industry we can use some tools such as the Five Forces and the Value Chain, by Michael Porter, as well as the description of the business model of that industry.

The value chain can provide information to perform the following tasks:

- To serve as a basis for determining the business model
- Identify sources of competitive advantage that are often discreetly distributed throughout the company.
- Align interests with customers and suppliers
- Clarify, together with Ansoff's analysis, the convenience of vertical integration or diversification by segments, geographies or industries
- Identify interrelations with other companies, seek alliances or design barriers to entry
- Presents a matrix of nine crossed categories, allowing the identification of areas for improvement.

It is interesting to perform this analysis per business unit, not at the company level in its entirety. The level of detail can be very high and in this way points of continuous improvement can be identified as they collect the theories based on Kaizen or Blue Ocean, on specific problems.

Finally we would study the macro environment, through the well-known SPLET analysis that is an acronym formed of the elements that integrate it, social, political, legal, economic, technological, and others. This can be complemented with a scenario analysis creating a matrix composed of two axes, one of which is the possible scenarios (of opportunities and threats) with their probability of occurrence and the other the impact they would have on our company. Within the matrix, we would write the actions to be taken in the case of the hypothetical scenarios given.

MATRIX of Opportunities and Threats	HIGH	Probability		LOW
HIGH Importance LOW	SCENARIO 1 Description of scenario and actions required			

For example, if I am going to start a business to sell wind power generators for domestic users, I will have studied the environment and measured the potential segments and once this is done I can then think of a series of scenarios that produce changes in that environment in order to be prepared in advance. A scenario could consist of legislative changes that prevent me from selling the generated energy or even connecting to the electricity grid. Another scenario could be a change in the prices of fossil fuels that make my product more or less profitable. A third scenario could be the emergence of cheaper or more efficient solar technologies that change my product's positioning. Using the matrix of opportunities and threats, we can anticipate the facts, evaluate them and design responses to adapt to changes in the environment.

All this situational analysis will generate a lot of information and when done in a cyclical way, will show us trends, propitiate ideas and generate improvements in the way of governing our business. Normally, after carrying out the situational analysis, the resulting data will be consolidated and studied using a SWOT analysis. In order to do this, it is necessary to collect this data as it occurs. I propose that you use a template like the one attached below to capture the information that will emerge when you use the tools indicated above.

Each time you use one of the environment analysis tools, you will identify **opportunities, threats, strengths and weaknesses**. Write them up at that time, relate them to the offer you are designing and capture the ideas related to innovation, differentiation, the objectives pursued and the actions necessary to achieve them. In this way, when you finish the situational analysis you will have made a lot of advance headway. We will review these concepts later.

RESULTS PER TOOL					
OFFERING	SWOT Components (S,W,O,T)	Aspects of INNOVATION	Aspects of DIFFERENTIATION	OBJECTIVES	ACTIONS

10 STRATEGY AS A PROCESS

As we have begun to see, strategy is a diffuse concept that we must define in order to work with it. In addition, defining it will help us improve communication within the company, which is one of the bases of innovation. We all know that we have to improve our strategy but we will barely achieve anything if we do not know what we are talking about.

The definitions and tools that we will use will be classic and widely known, **but endowing them with a procedural approach is where the value will be**.

We will start from the classic strategy model defined by Michael Porter in his historical book "Competitive Advantage", and his concept of differentiation. I will not go into explaining these concepts because they are sufficiently publicised and can be widely found. Just remember that there are three generic strategies that generate competitive advantage, the price, the niche market and the differentiation. The advantage in prices is a dangerous strategy since there will only be one winner. The niche strategy is difficult to find because of the small size of the market, although if it has already been found it will have to be maintained because it is difficult for competitors to enter there. Therefore, the biggest strategy to develop is that of differentiation because of the huge potential that it presents, only limited by our imagination. Up to this point everything is familiar territory.

Therefore, the fundamental component of strategy is differentiation. It is necessary to create different products and services to put them onto the market. But who in the company is responsible for seeking this required differentiation? This is where the problems start.

There are many theoretical tools and management models to look into and use for areas of improvement, from the proposals in the book by M. Porter in the Value Chain, to the ideas developed in the book by W. Chan Kim and Renée Mauborgne and Blue Ocean Strategy. Each one is either easier or more difficult to use. However, there is one basic but necessary concept to generate differentiation; this is the concept of innovation. Innovation is a process that provides ideas to differentiate the company in the market through its incorporation into products, services and business models. Innovation is the process on which strategy is built.

11 THE MARKETING STRATEGY SYNTHETIC MODEL

In order to easily manage the concept of strategy, we will use a model that we will refer to as the **Marketing Strategy Synthetic Model** (MSSM® 2016 Hugo Rubio) introduced in this book. The model combines the components of strategy synthetically and procedurally, placing them in relation to the other components of the marketing plan.

The **MSSM®** is fed by the data from the previous situational analysis that every company must perform in a constant and permanent way. This is the case since the environment is also in permanent flux; this means we must adjust to it (I do not say adapt but adjust; sometimes you have to be disruptive and change the environment) modifying our strategy. We will never be safe and therefore we must review and question everything permanently and constantly. *The great philosopher Karl Popper said that 'he man who is sure of something adopts the position of the madman'.* The madman does not reason. The man sure of something is not safe either because in his certainty, he does not feel the need to question or reason out anything. The SOSTAC® model, since it is cyclical does not give rise to absolute security, as it is permanently renewing itself.

The MSSM® is, as its name suggests, is a synthetic model, but at the same time it is very rich. It incorporates a lot of information regarding data and processes. **The purpose is to have the model in mind as an agile tool to manage and communicate our ideas**. An easy-to-use strategy model facilitates communication within the company and helps to exchange ideas. If we use it in our company as a conceptual framework we can communicate better and waste less time on sterile discussions about what is important and what is not (everything is important, in time and in the right order). We must remember that **the process of innovation, essential in today's world, begins with a sound internal communication process**.

The MSSM® synthesises the process of the strategy and is in turn the entry point for the tactics. A tactical implementation cannot be made if the result of the strategy is weak or not well understood. If, for example, we want to hire a marketing agency to design a communication plan, we must first inform the agency of the results of our strategy so that with this knowledge the agency can develop an effective plan. The same product could have different strategic components assigned to different companies that would lead to totally different tactical plans. It is necessary to clearly define this concept.

An example could be the case of the design and marketing of a steel watch. A certain brand, such as Rolex, could want to place it as a luxury item and provide specific differentiating components for a specific target that would materialize in a specific position. From here, a tactical plan (the 7 Ps) would be developed for this strategy. Another company, such as Seiko, with a similar product, could assign other differentiating factors to another target and achieve another positioning that would lead to another tactical plan. And all this for a product that is conceptually very similar (a mechanical steel watch) whose differentiating components cannot be understood if you are not introduced to the subject (just ask someone who is not a fan of watch making to explain the differences between them, except for the price). Implementing a tactic (the 7 Ps) without a clear and explicit strategy makes little sense and is a candidate for failure.

Let's start with the description of strategy's components. We need to remember once again that strategy is a process, not a static concept and that it encompasses several components, some of which are also processes. The components of strategy will be analysed in more detail later.

Analysing and understanding the market is a complicated task. Satisfying it by creating differentiation is not easy either. To do so it is necessary to generate ideas, business ideas, product and process improvement alongside communication with customers. We are talking about **INNOVATION**.

Innovation is the fundamental pillar of strategy. Differentiation will be fed by what innovation generates. Without innovation there will be no differentiation. In your company there has to be an innovation process. You can start smoothly with innovation, it is not necessary to have an R&D department. We will develop these ideas later.

Innovation then feeds **DIFFERENTIATION:** this is the central component of strategy. This concept is the holy grail of marketing. It was defined by M. Porter (and previously by J. Schumpeter) many years ago within the concept of generic strategies (niche, cost and differentiation) and is still the most problematic point to solve. We must seek to be different by adding value and, above all, not get stuck in the middle, without giving enough value, or being able to compete on prices.

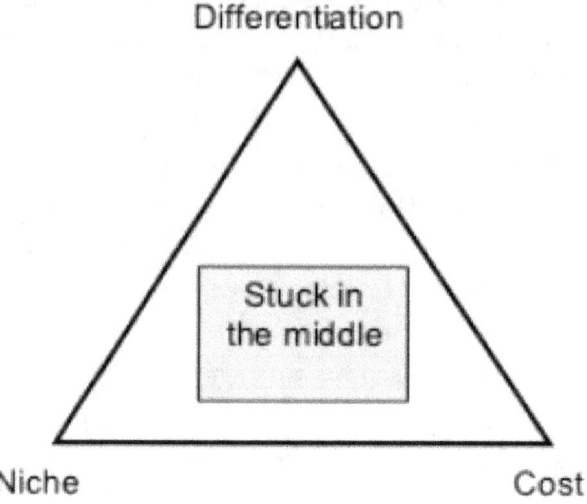

It is not about being the best, there will only ever be one who fills that slot (just as there will always be one that is cheapest). You have to be different from competitors, for the segment (target) that you have chosen. This is where the next component of strategy, the **TARGET**, is introduced.

Segmenting the market is something that we usually do infrequently and badly. It is a difficult but essential task. We will talk about that later. Companies implement differentiation in their products or services, but talking about a product in this phase would condition us significantly. When we talk about a product we are already defining it. In this phase of the strategy, the product or service is in the definition phase according to the target, which may also be in the process of identification. It could also be a product, a service, a product line, a family of products, an increase in product attributes or all of these. To avoid this problem of definition we will call it **OFFERING** (instead of product), which includes all these possibilities, without detailing them.

To illustrate this concept of OFFERING we can give the example of offering the cinema experience via internet. The client could acquire different types of receivers, such as a hard disk drive, a memory key type, computer-based or mobile devices. At the same time customers could benefit from different types of services, basic, premium or video store service. All this would evolve with the needs of the market. This is basically an offering, as opposed to a product. In fact, an offering can be maintained by changing the products that make it up.

So, we have an **OFFERING-TARGET set** that will be the core of the strategy. Normally, when we come up with business ideas, these come in the form of duality: product (or solution) - client (or need). It does not matter what happened first, the customer-need or the product-solution, but it is very difficult for us to come up with one without the other.

This set is the centre of the strategy. Almost all the situational analysis that is normally consolidated in the SWOT analysis amounts to responding to the need to identify what our client wants (opportunities-threats) and how to satisfy it with our offering (strengths-weaknesses). What our target wants is, summarized in one word, the WHAT (what do you want). What we will give you is summarized in another, the HOW (how we satisfy that what). We will return to these concepts later.

We already have four components of strategy, innovation, which nurtures differentiation, contained in the offering, which satisfies our target. All this leads us to be able to occupy a place in the market where we are seen or as we want to be seen (sometimes we are seen as we do not want to be). **POSITIONING** has two sides: a) where we want to position ourselves and b) where the market positions us. It is very difficult and expensive (it is strategic) to change the positioning of a company. If it goes down in its positioning perceived by the market it will be extremely difficult to go back up. We may well have a good offer but remain unseen in the market in our desired position.

Choosing the desired POSITIONING obviously requires having identified the TARGET and DIFFERENTIATED our OFFERING, based in turn on INNOVATION. For now, these are the components of strategy. However, there is a problem; all this is worthless if our customers do not see our positioning. We have to make sure that our target sees us (literally as opposed to figuratively with their own eyes). Here, communication will play a fundamental role. We will call this strategic communication, to differentiate it from the tactical activity described in the media plan, **POSITIVE CUSTOMER PERCEPTION** (or negative, if we are not successful). If the client does not see us, we do not exist and our entire strategy will simply not materialise in the marketplace.

These six components form the marketing strategy. **Innovation** is a process that **differentiates** our **offering**. The **target** is a concept that emerges from the segmentation process. **Positioning** is a concept that consolidates the previous ones and that in turn has to be **perceived in a positive way** by the market. If any of these components fail, is not well developed or is not consistent with the rest, you have a strategic problem that must be identified and solved as soon as possible to avoid incurring higher expenses, decreasing income or temporary delays.

From now on, if someone were to ask you what your company strategy should be, you should have a well-developed discourse that encompasses all six concepts. Explaining your strategy will take time, if you have done it, of course!

The strategy developed in a company materializes in what is

known as competitive advantage. Competitive advantage is another concept that is difficult to identify but that must be defined and audited in the design phase of the strategy. Our strategy obviously has to generate competitive advantage. We will dedicate an entire chapter to this concept.

Once our strategy is established, we will implement it with the tactics, the well-known 7 Ps. Each group of 7 Ps belonging to a OFFERING-TARGET set is known as Marketing Mix or MMIX. I will not tire of differentiating these two concepts. **We have to know how to identify on the go when we are talking about strategy and when tactics and never confuse them**. Thus, our strategy will generate OFFERING-TARGET sets, with its own competitive advantage that will be released to the market in the form of MMIX, one MMIX for each set. The OFFERING-TARGET sets are defined in the strategic phase. The MMIX provides the detail in the tactical phase, during which it will be physically created.

It is key to clearly understand when we are working in OFFERING / TARGET mode (strategy) and when we working in PRODUCT (tactical) mode. Day to day we will occupy our time dedicated mostly to working in product mode, its details, the range, product families and other diverse attributes, forgetting the strategic analysis. This is one of the biggest causes of strategic drift and its fatal consequences.

Step 1: Generate. Do you have one?	**INNOVATION PROCESS**
Step 2: Create, by innovating	**DIFFERENTIATION** The "**HOW**". **OFFERING** design, composed by product, services and attributes, and by the business model and its processes.
Step 3: Identify.	**SEGMENTATION and TARGETING** The "**WHAT**", obtained by analysing the customer decision process.
Step 4: Check. (Do you have it?)	**COMPETITIVE ADVANTAGE AUDIT** (using the QFD tool)
Step 5: Obtain. (Is it the desired one?)	**POSITIONING**
Step 6: Check. Is the customer perceiving what you designed?	**CUSTOMER PERCEPTION** The "**WHY**", strategic communication
Proceed to TACTICS	MMIX generation

The MARKETING STRATEGY SYNTHETIC MODEL (MSSM®).

Notice that the six steps don't correspond directly with the six components of the model. Components of the model are **1.- Innovation process, 2.- differentiation, 3.- offering design, 4.- targeting (implicates segmentation), 5.- positioning and 6.- customer perception**. Step 4, competitive advantage audit, is not a component, but a method to understand if our offering design is competitive enough. Step 2, includes two components of the model.

This model processes a lot of information. Its importance lies in how this information flows coherently from data collection to tactical implementation through the concept of strategy. We will explain the various components of the model below. While we are doing it, you can contrast, if in your particular case, the model allows you to find points of failure or areas of improvement.

Do not start with the tactical plan (the generation of 7 Ps for each MMIX) before having a clear and defined strategy process outlined in the MSSM®. If you do, you will probably incur serious errors, the resolution of which will exhaust your time and resources, preventing you even from going back to the design phase. **Remember that strategy is design while tactics is the implementation of that design.**

11.1 STRATEGIC DRIFT

It is important to identify that if we neglect our strategic development we could easily fall into what is known as strategic drift.

This concept aims to convey the following: Lack of clear and effective distinction between tactical and strategic actions and results can make us believe that we are making strategic decisions, when in reality we are only working tactically. The result is that in a slow and barely perceptible manner, the company begins a drift that distances it from the correct strategic positioning. When you finally realise this, the situation may be too late to rectify due to the deadlines and resources involved in these types of decisions. This happens frequently because once certain strategic actions are implemented organisations relax and dedicate their time to making small tactical changes. We rest on our laurels so to speak.

That is why it is so important to perform a thorough situation analysis, supported by tools that help us to correctly determine the problem. If we have a strategic problem but instead identify a tactical one, we will have made an error of the so-called Type 3 errors. From that moment, we will dedicate our time and resources to solving without identifying the true cause and the strategic problem will remain unsolved. We will have fallen into a strategic drift.

Remember that our strategy fails when the client does not see our positioning (negative customer perception) or when the segment does not want what we offer (wrong OFFERING-TARGET set). Paradoxically, it may be easier to create a good OFFERING-TARGET set than to achieve the desired positioning in the market. We all know many cases in which the image of a company or brand still has a strong position in the minds of customers due to their history or on the contrary, how difficult it can be to open a gap in the market even when our product is better than that of the competitors, because we are not known.

Therefore, to avoid falling into the strategic drift, we must keep our INNOVATION process active in our company, guaranteeing that it generates enough DIFFERENTIATION for our TARGET or groups of targets, that we occupy the desired POSITION in our market, and that all of this is PERCEIVED POSITIVELY by our customers.

One of the most interesting cases of strategic drift that has happened recently is that of the company KODAK. The company had a great strategy centred on products and services around the processes of photography and treatment of images with chemical basis. In the end, it was a company in the chemical sector. Many of its directors were chemical engineers busy looking for efficiencies in complicated production and development processes. It also had good tactical deployment, with stores and franchises in all cities and neighbourhoods, a striking logo and a name that could be pronounced in all languages.

With the advent of digital cameras the market changed. KODAK chemical engineers did not understand the digital computer industry. They thought they were two different worlds, but that was not the case. As a result, KODAK began its strategic drift. Their customers stopped seeing them since they could now avoid the costly chemical development service.

Because the company had strong tactics they survived albeit languishing for many years. Longer term they were not able to generate a substitute strategy and finally the company went bankrupt in 2012. Many of the solutions that they tried to launch on the market were tactical, based around the industry where they positioned. However, its TARGET was already thinking about another type of OFFERING.

The opposite case is also possible, when you have the right strategy but bad tactical implementation. In this case a company survives but with difficulty. These cases tend to occur when the product is good and there is a market. However, inappropriate management of the family of products due to excessive supply, confusion between options, overlapping of products, management costs and communication errors, to give some examples, begin to negatively affect the financial returns of the company and even damage its positioning in the market.

Drift and strategic exhaustion	Correct STRATEGY Incorrect	
Correct **TACTICS**	**BUSINESS SUCCESS**	**SLOW FAILURE**
Incorrect	**SURVIVES WITH DIFFICULTY**	**FAILURE**

Awareness of a problem is almost half of the solution. On the contrary, if we are unaware, we will never solve it.

11.2 INNOVATION AND DIFFERENTIATION

The concept of innovation seems modern and is nowadays used widely although in fact, it really is very old. Its modern usage is attributed to J. Schumpeter, an economist born in the 1880s in Prussia. In his books, genuine ideas are set out about the concept of differentiation. His ideas were later intelligently developed by M. Porter.

Schumpeter is known as being the father of the concept of **"creative destruction"** according to which, it is necessary to break and destroy what has gone before in order to give way to the new which will emerge with renewed strength. This idea already existed in the collective subconscious and is transmitted in the form of stories and legends such as the phoenix, the universal flood or the crossing of the desert. The old disappears and the new arises creating a new paradigm, or frame of reference.

Everyone wants to differentiate but this is not possible without innovation, hence its importance. On the other hand, the innovation process is very simple, it is based on three components: generation of ideas, evaluation of these ideas generated by selecting those considered valuable, and the dissemination of the results.

But this process needs to be implemented within the company. It is interesting to note that both **strategy and its components are processes**. This means that they must be implemented and maintained in the company through methodologies which capacitate people. In the end they are integrated into the company through cultural change and in turn change the culture of the company.

It is much better to innovate through cultural change rather than through ad hoc procedures. Setting out to innovate is difficult since we are looking for something new; it will be difficult to identify and even talk about it as it refers to something that does not exist yet. It is better to implement a process that provokes and picks up on innovation than to specifically seek it out.

Large companies have R&D, research and development departments. Some even have "inventors" in their teams. Small ones do not have any of this. But all companies have the most important asset for innovation: people and their knowledge.

The innovation model based on dedicated departments and centres is called the **"linear model"**. It has its purpose, obviously and works for what is intended. Another more integrative model does exist; **SECI** developed by Nonaka and Takeuchi in which participation is not only open to multiple participants but also it is also based on nurturing of the process. **SECI** is an acronym that means knowledge **socialization**, first within the company, spreading the tacit knowledge, which is often held and practiced but not integrated into an explicit procedure; **externalisation**, to communicate this knowledge to other groups and even outside the company; **combination**, with other types of knowledge from other sources that in turn have been outsourced and returned; **integration** to enrich the knowledge of the company explicitly.

This model implies that knowledge is distributed within the company, from the employees. Everyone can and should contribute to the process. Ideas do not occur to us when we organize a meeting for that purpose, but all the time, at any time. The sessions called "brainstorming" are usually poorly planned; encouraging people to say whatever comes to mind instead of ideas of value. **Ideas of value arise when we combine sound knowledge of a situation, good industrial knowledge, solid contextual knowledge and appropriate methodology**.

For this methodology to be effective, it must be given a high profile through internal communication, making it participatory and visible and through sharing its results. The internal communication plan in the company is very important and is sometimes terribly neglected. The internal communication plan can be the first component to implement a process of solid innovation in the company. The implementation of the SOSTAC® methodology can facilitate this process, establishing a common language to identify areas of improvement in the company. In this manner, planning goes from being a descriptive and passive activity to an analytical one, active and generating ideas.

I have a friend who says that we spend a lot of time working. It's funny when he says it but he's quite right. Time is wasted when we work on 'auto pilot' instead of fully devoting ourselves, for example, to thinking. We waste the opportunity cost of that time, when it could have been dedicated to tasks of greater interest. Working has different degrees!

I usually tell my university students not to give me great ideas in their coursework. I'm not going to give high grades for those ideas that I am really not able to evaluate, but for the use of the methodology I teach them. That is the purpose of my subject.

Methodology is fundamental, but then in real life we must complement it with ideas, good ideas, and great ideas if we are capable of generating them. In this case, my students are right. Often good management in our work performance, in addition to the basis of sound methodology contributes to generating that good idea, that light bulb moment that appears as if out of nowhere, that quick response to a client's need, or the sudden realization that something can be improved upon or when a good opportunity shows up and you grab it.

This idea that produces good management will arise if we are prepared, if we know the environment, the situation, the methodology, in short, if we look proactively. Therefore, a great idea that can occur to us at any given moment may have value, but it will rarely be sustainable. Companies that succeed in the long term do so because they have methodologies that lead to the generation of ideas, the conversion of ideas into products and services and the correct perception of their customers. The methodology and its implementation are important.

Ideas do not only apply to products. We are normally very oriented to thinking about products but we must also think about markets, customers, business models, expansion areas, alliances, processes, channels, in short, everything that affects the business. It is worth highlighting the fact that that the result of innovation is destined to populate the first quadrant of the BCG matrix, that of the questions. New ideas give rise to new offerings. In turn, the axes of the BCG matrix must also be objects of innovation. Before launching innovative ideas for products, it is necessary to determine whether the object of our innovation coincides with the growing market, stands out from the competition or is akin to the capabilities of the company. By innovating, entire markets can be changed, as is the example of music in electronic format. Music remains the same (the basic product) but the industry and its dynamics have changed completely, just as the book industry is doing.

In your company, establish a procedure that allows employees to generate ideas. Reward them for doing it. Explain the process to them; prepare them so that they know that only a few ideas will be finally implemented but that this should not be an obstacle to proposals or cause frustration. Many ideas will not prosper but will serve as a basis to generate others that will. I have been able to verify this fact over the years. In this way, a culture of innovation will be generated. Certain internal competition may be necessary, but not much. Too much internal competition produces individualism and, as a consequence, it stops collaboration and can turn into an opportunity instead of gaining an advantage over one's peers. Remember that the wild competition, Darwinism, the survival of the fittest, will be taken care of by the market itself. Within the company we will not do this. An organization, in which a Darwinian ethos reigns, does not need directors. It is better to create a culture of collaboration since this leads to sharing of knowledge as is encouraged following the SECI model. Remember that innovation is based on culture, the style of the company and this has to be created, it does not arise spontaneously nor is it based on individualistic behaviours. In turn, the ideas generated must be valued against the capabilities, strengths and opportunities of the company and produce improvements in the form of new products, services, processes or business models. Finally, the BCG matrix must show those new products and services prepared to start their commercial life.

This way, we will keep our offer alive, modified in a dynamic and participatory manner. I have met directors who prioritized the need to convey their strategy to all employees and in turn collect their ideas. I have met others who felt that it is not necessary to communicate everything to everyone. The important thing is to detect the existing need and be able to respond using a well articulated plan and methodology to collect ideas. To what extent it will be necessary to extend it in the organization will depend on each particular case.

Very often during the work sessions that I carry out with companies for the implementation of this methodology, someone will remark that "Something must be going right in the company, since the business is going well" and they are quite correct. But the problem lies precisely in not knowing what is done well. Tacit knowledge is possessed, but you have to transform it into explicit knowledge, identify what is done well, process it, write it down, improve it and use it to build a competitive advantage. If the business is going well there is no problem. However, when it starts to go wrong due to a change in the environment (and the environment always does change) we will not know what we are doing wrong, just as we did not know what we used to do well before. This problem is very common in family businesses, when the successive generations that govern the company lose touch with the deep knowledge of the business strategy and replace it with a technical and financial administration.

11.3 DESIGN OF THE OFFERING

The offering, as we have previously seen, is an idea that will later be transformed into a product or family of products together with its services. It is, obviously, the first step towards generating differentiation. By calling it an offering we intend to expand on the possibilities we have of materialisation and thus avoid becoming prisoners of our own product. This is known as **Marketing Myopia**, a term coined by Theodore Levitt in the 1960s. I recommend you browse the internet for this reference and read his famous article, Marketing Myopia.

The underlying message is that products satisfy the wishes or needs of the customers. The product is the materialisation of the offering but will change, even in its concept. A few years ago in the United States, I saw an old lounge radio, a wooden device, voluminous and beautifully designed. The brand was Zenith. Looking through the grilles on its back, I could see the vacuum valves made by Motorola. Later Zenith designed and manufactured many other electronic devices. Motorola, for its part, continued to manufacture components and consolidated itself as one of the largest manufacturers of microprocessors: from a Zenith radio with Motorola valves to a Zenith computer with Motorola processors. Not only do products change, but also the motives and requirements which can totally transform the company. Nokia started as a footwear company and consolidated itself years later as a communications technology manufacturer.

Because of this, our offering must be linked to what our target wants and not vice versa. On too many occasions we undertake a business project because we do what we have done all our lives, whether it is inheriting a family business that makes a certain product, liking something in particular and channelling our business energy there, doing what we do or what we know, or on the contrary, lacking knowledge which limits the possibilities and therefore we do what we can.

It is true that we must undertake business projects based on our knowledge. But the reciprocal is not true. That is, business projects should not condition our knowledge. Instead, our knowledge should adapt to market opportunities. All this may seem very obvious, but it is a great source of mistakes in strategy.

Let's give some examples. I really like triathlons, I am very fond of them and I understand the sport. It occurred to me that I could set up a store to sell triathlon material.

This is a very typical example many people have done it, adapting it to their specific circumstances. The business mistake is not to set up the store because you like that particular sport but set up the store of a sport in growth and develop the knowledge that business requires.

To do what your father did and what your grandfather did, is a romantic idea but is fundamentally weak in business terms. If you are lucky enough to work in a profitable and sustainable market segment and have exclusive knowledge, great, but always remain proactively alert to changes in the market.

If you have training in a specific discipline but there is no demand for it, you have to develop new knowledge. If you have studied journalism (to give a real example) but the market is saturated, you should urgently complement your career with other knowledge that does have demand.

If you lack differentiating knowledge, you have to be extremely cautious. Starting a business of any kind, conditioned by the lack of knowledge is one of the reasons that 90% of the businesses that are start up fail.

On many occasions, the offer will be similar among the different competitors. You can see in the market, that whether you talk about clothes or computers, different brands offer a basic product (trousers, a computer) that materializes in the market through product lines or families. From the base product others develop consisting of additional characteristics (types, benefits) as well as services (guarantees, facilities and others). The detail of the increased product and its service components corresponds to the tactic, although its design must be contemplated in the strategy. The more differentiation the offer has in its strategic design, the less dependence we will have on its tactical details. A car is a car, but Tesla's and Renault's offerings (for example and without comparison) are clearly differentiated and compete differently in different market segments. A screw manufacturer will find it much more difficult to differentiate their base product and may have to compete on price.

When you design the offering, consider the possibilities that the base product gives you, what attributes you can confer on it to generate an increased product and what service components you can equip it with so that all this generates the necessary differentiation that your segment demands.

Remember that the mistakes you make here will not be able to be corrected in the tactical phase when the product is already defined. In the same way that once you have decided that you are going to manufacture a Renault Twizy there is no way to transform it into a Tesla model S (or reverse). It is not a problem of the design of a car (tactical) but a problem of not having understood the requirements of the market and, consequently, to err in the definition of the offering and its materialization in the product. To avoid this, we would have to redesign the strategy (and, of course, have to of correctly understood the market requirements).

A company must generate, using innovation, different sets of offering-target. Many of them will fail, but some will triumph. We should not be afraid of failed proposals (as long as they do not ruin us, of course). This manual on strategy aims precisely for the approach of these offering-target sets to be as accurate as possible. ***As Einstein said, 'The best way to generate a good idea is to*** *generate many'*. However I would say, with Einstein's permission that alongside methodology and preparation the proportion of good ideas will be greater.

The ideas generated, in the form of offering-target sets, will be incorporated into our product portfolio. Our product portfolio should always have products in several quadrants, as indicated by the analysis tool known as the Boston matrix, or BCG matrix. This is the well known matrix of cows, stars, dogs and question marks. I will not explain it here since it is well known. For any product of ours to become a star or a cow, it will first have to be a question mark. Many questions, around ninety percent will go to the wall. That is the reality, so it is necessary that our innovation process allows the agile design of concepts, prototypes and real products and that we are able to contemplate their programmed failure with the least possible damage to the company.

Our offerings must follow the cycle from question marks to stars and then to cows, in a significant percentage. Otherwise, our strategy is not working. The matrix must reflect a dynamic equilibrium.

MATRIX BCG	+ PENETRATION IN THE MARKET -	
	Stars: These are the offerings that have been successful. They finance their own growth.	**Question Marks:** This is where the offering is generated. This quadrant must be sufficiently filled with new offerings derived from the innovation process. Consume resources.
HIGHER **GROWTH IN THE MARKET**		
LOWER	**Cows:** They are ancient stars. The market no longer grows but we have no competitors, so the product is very profitable. Finance the generation of new offerings.	**Dogs:** Many of the offerings will fall to this quadrant because the market has declined and are no longer interesting. Consume resources.

In addition to the BCG and even before, we must analyse how our company as a whole fits into the market we want to serve. The activities that we develop will be conditioned by this decision and therefore will condition our strategy. Once an activity has started, it will be very difficult to change to another, but we will be able to bring it back in a sustained manner according to the changes in the environment.

For this the GE Matrix (General Electric) or directional matrix can help us. In one of its axes we will locate what attracts us from a market or an industry. In the other, we will show how our company adapts to it. Notice that this is very similar to the opportunities and strengths of the SWOT. This is precisely where this data comes from (remember to consolidate this in the template for Chapter 9).

Once the matrix is configured, we must choose markets (opportunities) and develop strengths to serve them, through training and innovation.

The GE Matrix is about balancing our strengths with opportunities. This is not obvious; in fact, often we find ourselves giving value to doing something that we want over and above another option that may be more convenient. A typical case is the choice of studies for our professional career. What do we do? What we like or what will allow us to get a job? It is a very common discussion for which there is no direct answer. I have seen defence of the two positions with good arguments.

This tool helps us evaluate and ponder. The choice of my professional career was a hard decision for me, as it usually is for everyone. The world of engineering interested me a lot, although I was not sure I had the required skills. Later, once I completed my University studies, I used to advise other people who were also in doubt, about studying engineering. A good friend, whom I hold in high esteem, once told me not to give advice, that could confuse people and that it is better for each person to decide for themselves. I never understood why he didn't follow his own advice but I listened to him and I spent a long time without giving direct advice. If someone asked me I would respond with an approach based on the directional matrix, with which the interested person could clarify their doubts a little.

Advising has its risks. It is true that you can cause confusion, but being aware of this, you can minimise the risk. You may also find that your advice is even criticised. Because of this, it is wise to set a scenario of possibilities leaving the decision to the interested party, making it appear that the decision depends on several components that have to be weighed up.

GE MATRIX or Directional	+ BUSINESS ATTRACTIVENESS -			
Higher **BUSINESS CAPACITY** **Lower**				

Oriental cultures try to avoid these discussions with their famous philosophy based on yin and yang. Everything has two sides. It is about accepting that and looking for a point of equilibrium, even if this point is mobile on almost all occasions. If you do what you like, clearly you will do better, but without neglecting the objective you are pursuing. It will always be easier to do what we like and we will do it better, although in many cases we will have to do what we do not like.

This has some correlation with the famous concept of Comparative Advantage, introduced by the great economist David Ricardo in the face of the modern concept of Competitive Advantage. Comparative advantage occurs when we do something easier or cheaper than others. A country may have a comparative advantage in labour, in access to resources or in having certain knowledge. This could figure on the axis of strengths. Nevertheless, additionally, competitive advantage could be developed to acquire other strengths that we do not yet have and in this way we can pursue new opportunities. You can have a geographical area where vine cultivation is good (a comparative advantage) and also develop knowledge to produce and market excellent wine (competitive advantage). You can have comparative advantage for the tourism industry since you have sun and beaches, but want to develop competitive advantage in the industrial and technological sector.

The GE Matrix allows us to explore all these concepts at different levels of analysis. Opportunities should be broadly analysed at the level of industry, market, offering level or product level if we have reached this level of definition. That is why I have called the horizontal axis "Business Attractiveness", so that it can be replaced by industry, market, offering or product / segment, among others. That is to say, the Attractiveness of the Business can be broken down as follows:

1. **Attractiveness of the industry** of which we are part. For example, we could be a computer company dedicated to hardware and we decide to switch to software as it grows more. We would be in the software industry.

2. **Attractiveness of the client industry (market)**. We could decide what we are going to focus on, for example, clients from a certain sector, such as the Banking sector. Many companies are organised by industries in a way that they can better adapt and understand in detail the needs of their customers. This also allows us to raise the level of dialogue with the client and improve communication and positioning of our company.

3. **Attractiveness of the Offering**. In this step, we start with designing the offering, conditioned by our industry and the client's own industry. Remember that the offering is the first thing that the customer sees and that it is made up of products that can be modified. For example, Netflix sells cinema at home, on demand. It started by renting DVDs by mail and today it does it online. Additionally, it has created new offerings such as the production of its own series.

4. **Attractiveness of the product**. Here we develop the com-

ponents of the offering according to the needs of the customer segments, which must be studied in detail as will be seen in the corresponding chapter.

This analysis will allow us to better understand the client and establish a higher level of dialogue. By trying to better understand the industry in which a client operates, we improve our level of knowledge and interlocution. It is necessary to avoid talking about our product until we have made space for the client to talk about their own, their industry, their needs and their associated problems.

Before trying to sell something you have to understand what the client wants and this procedure will help you. Allow the client to tell you, practice active listening; do not interrupt with your comments until he/she finishes talking. Demonstrate real interest in their problems, be as assertive as you can and your offer will have greater chances of success in that industry since it will incorporate the needs that your clients have indicated in their design. When you have the opportunity to talk about your product do it with the perspective of the industry and look for the advantages it brings in accordance with the value chain of the client and its industry.

Note that the BCG and GE matrices can be put in correspondence since normally the business that will attract us most (horizontal axis of the GE matrix) will coincide with the growing market (vertical axis of the BCG matrix). I say this because all too often, these tools are not applied with sufficient coherence and therefore do not get their full potential. These analytical tools are already classic and quite simple but using them well can contribute many ideas to our business.

In the example we have seen, we would select only the businesses that appear shaded in the matrix and that match our capabilities. That is to say that there will be businesses that interest us less but for which we have a lot of capacity and vice versa. The interesting thing about this study is that it forces us to recognize the businesses that interest us in the future and adapt our capabilities to them.

The directional matrix is the beginning of the strategic analysis that will allow us to begin with the design of the offering-target set. It is a simple concept but of great significance and not always clearly identified. So much so that the European Union has launched its smart specialization program RIS3 within its Europe 2020 program to encourage the regions to explicitly identify their opportunities and capabilities, thus generating competitive and sustainable regional strategies. Companies have business strategies, but regions and countries too. You must be successful in identifying your opportunities as well as developing the corresponding capabilities.

11.4 THE BUSINESS MODEL

The business model is the second concept, after the design of the offering, which allows us to continue generating differentiation. The business model is a much more abstract concept than the concept of offering. It is not easy to identify a business model and even less to use it specifically for differentiating for our company.

We must begin by saying that a company's business model is conditioned by the generic business model of the industry in which it operates (and in which our competitors therefore operate) and by the client's business model. Therefore there will be opportunities for improvement both in our own model and in the way in which our model connects with that of the client. The changes that occur in our customer's business model will lead to changes in the business model of our industry and vice versa.

For example, changes in the families' lifestyle habits (client's business model) produce changes in the way in which the food industry meets the needs of families both in the way they produce food, package and conserve it, facilitate preparation at home, increase the offer of meals away from home or catering at home.

There are some tools that aim to help with the problem of identifying and improving business models. The most classic comes from M. Porter, and are the Value Chain and the Five Forces. I will not explain these models here because they are well known and widely disseminated but I will encourage you to use them in order to improve your internal processes and therefore the business model.

Perhaps the most useful thing to understand this is to start by setting out the processes that affect our company with the basic scheme of boxes and arrows. There are tools on the market to model processes and others to implement them by computer. Before modelling you have to understand what happens in the market, how industries work and identify your points of improvement. Once this is done, we can better model our own processes. You can search the internet for images of the value chain or business models of companies or industries. It will be very illustrative.

Let's use an example. Think of a traditional restaurant that wants to increase its business. The traditional model is to attract and serve customers on the premises. At its most simplified, this model requires a suitable place, a kitchen, cooks and waiting staff. The restaurant wants to add a new model to its business consisting of cooking and delivering food to customers at home. This would require a means of transport, owned or rented capability to package and present food and some increase in production capacity.

Another restaurant could think of something similar but with the business model slightly weighted towards catering for food at home. It could be a pizza type business. This model aims to attract certain customers but does not want to serve food on the premises more than necessary. Therefore, the place will not need be quite so pleasant, it could even be a bit uncomfortable in order for customers to place the order, eat and leave as soon as possible (thereby increasing turnover). The kitchen would look more like a production line than a traditional kitchen. On the other hand, the part of the model related to home delivery will be highly developed and that part will have a great weight for the positioning of the company in the market.

A third company could also plan home delivery of food, further improving the part of the model that refers to the delivery and the customer's own management. For this, it will focus on establishing relationships with suppliers that provide the food already cooked and even its deliver. This company has no premises, kitchen or processes related to it. It is limited to managing the order. The business model of this company focuses on the management of customers and suppliers as well as a broad geographical coverage that consolidates the desired positioning.

When a client is deciding where to eat something, he or she does not think about its possible suppliers' business model, but each one of these three companies will serve him/her based on a totally different model.

The business model does not necessarily have to be seen by the client. It can be, some companies promote this as part of their differentiation. For example, a bank may intend to approach the young segment by establishing different processes, perhaps based on new technologies and making them visible for that segment, while another may want to show traditional customers another type of process more in line with their needs, such as the direct management of their staff.

Additionally, there may be parts of the model that are not visible to customers but have a high impact on them. For example, a chain of fast food restaurants has a very visible model for the customer consisting of a standard meal (the customer knows what they will be served and what it will cost, there are no surprises), a place that is always clean and offers immediate service without a wait. The customer sees that part of the model but this is based on a part of the model that is not seen; consistency in logistics that ensure the products arrive in a way that guarantees speed, strict internal cooking processes and methodical preparation of their employees.

The business model and the design of the offering are the two main points to generate competitive advantage. The design of the offering is understood much more easily than the business model. The products and services are understood much better than the processes. Many innovative businesses rely more on business models than on products. They can even distort a market without changing the products, changing the balance of the forces of the industry.

For us, making the purchase in a supermarket is totally normal, but I remember the time when they did not exist and we made our purchases in the neighbourhood stores. The development of the superstores totally modified the market. Many small stores had to close down and relations between suppliers and customers (superstores) changed in favour of these. Actually, these mega stores do not sell anything that cannot be found in traditional stores. What changes is the model and sometimes it is something as simple as making a richer offer and an easier purchase available to customers, even though it is not necessarily cheaper.

In addition, superstores have implemented new models to generate income in addition to selling their products to the customer, such as the sale of shelf space, the volume discount, and the negative working capital (charging the customer before paying the supplier).

A similar example exists with the large international companies which sell furniture, clothing or sports. As soon as they open up, the existing business model in that geographical area is distorted due more to a model change than to a differentiation in product.

Think about your company's business models; consider which of them are client based and how they could be combined in a more suitable manner. As with the offering design, this will help identify what could be created, eliminated, improved or minimized; this must be done for internal and external processes.

The business model should be integrated into a broader planning tool. For example, SOSTAC® covers all areas of the marketing plan methodologically. CANVAS®, for its part, calls itself the tool for business model development; it is made up of almost the same components as SOSTAC®, presenting them in a more visual way although without the cyclical and sequential component. CANVAS® introduces the key processes that are a call to the generation of the business model. The MSSM® strategy model identifies the place where this component should be developed and aligned with the rest of the components of the strategy so that it can be incorporated into any planning process.

So, when you are going to think about how to improve your business model you can follow this script:

> 1.- Set the current model of your company using a box and arrow diagram, identifying the areas where the most value is contributed (strengths). You can identify these areas in the Porter Value Chain.
>
> 2.- Also draw up the industry model to understand the differences and similarities between our model and the generic industry (and that of our competitors).
>
> 3.- Draw the client's business model. Identify the points where the client receives the value (opportunities). This will be related to the customer's purchase process, explained later in the segmentation chapter.
>
> 4.- Also draw up the customer's industry model
>
> 5.- Identify opportunities by comparing these four models and place your offerings there. Identify how and where your client's model and your company's model connect. Identify how they differ from industry models and how you can adapt your model to the client's to create a competitive advantage.

Some cases of successful business models have triumphed by breaking into the market, altering their forces through important innovations. Some have been supported to a large extent by innovations in technology and others in exchange for proposing bold changes. As the great writer Bernard Shaw said, '***The reasonable man adapts himself to the world: the unreasonable one persists in trying to adapt the world to himself. Therefore, all progress depends on the unreasonable man***'.

Let's take a look at some examples of change in the business model:

- Small store / super store
- Bookstore / online store (Amazon)
- IKEA, does not offer only products, but lifestyle
- Bonuses, coupons and their adaptation to the internet
- Aggregators and comparison internet services
- Breakthrough design (Cirque du Soleil)
- Passive income, content generated by the client
- Advantageous cyclic contracting for both parties
- Genetically modified seeds (breakthrough change)

These changes in the business model produce changes, in the industry forces. The analysis of Porter's five forces allows us to visualize these changes. You can use the model dynamically, that is to say by reflecting changes in the industry.

We can also see how the forces of the software market change when modifying the way to market it, from product to service. Traditional suppliers lose strength. It is won by the substitutes that provide the service and new entrants that are already born with the new model. The market moves towards the new model.

Porter's 5 Forces Analysis

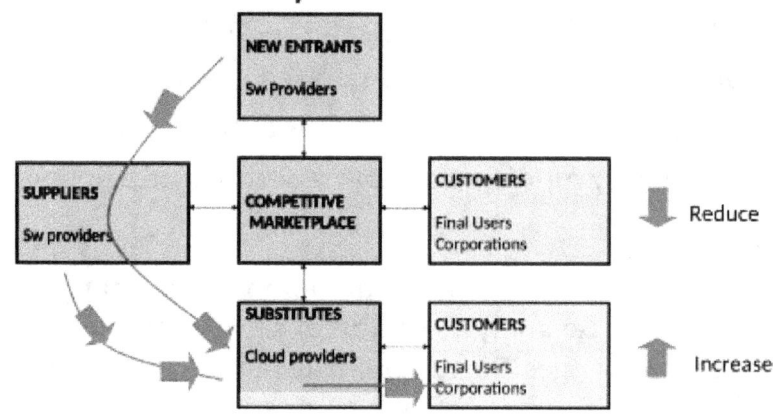

This method of analysing the business model together with the offering is a powerful generator of ideas that, if you recall, is the basis for feeding the strategic process. Ideas are generated better if we have the help of methodologies and tools. Take some time to apply these concepts to your particular problem and you will see how ideas for improvement arise both in products, services and in processes. Deepen your knowledge of the clients' world as much as possible.

11.5 SEGMENTATION AND TARGETING

The segmentation and targeting process provides the customer's point of view, their needs, desires and wishes. It is as important as it is difficult to put yourself in your client's shoes. Sometimes it is extremely difficult to admit that our product, that although better and cheaper than the competition, does not have the expected reception in the market. Understanding why this happens is the goal of strategic analysis.

The concept of segment and targeting is something that everyone knows about. A segment is a group of customers that has common or homogeneous characteristics for certain types of products or services and therefore has commercial interest. A target is a segment selected for the commercial action of our company because we can create products or services for it. It has the sufficient capacity for our business objectives, it is akin to the activity of our company and it is easily attainable along with other such arguments of this type. That is to say, there will be segments not considered as a target and towards which our company will not be directed (in order to simplify the nomenclature we will use the term "segment" instead of "target" once we have clarified what each one is). The segments of interest must be contained, in turn, within the markets or industries of interest to the company that are considered within the GE or directional matrix and that can be measured for the purposes of purchasing capacity.

This is very important because all too frequently we tend not to perform segmentation exercises. In such cases our product can end up being designed without sufficient differentiation or the communication strategy can be ineffective if it is not well targeted.

We previously reviewed the concept of MMIX and how it was made up of the 7 P's of marketing. The MMIX is developed on each offering defined in the strategic phase according to the selected segment (target) to which it is addressed. This is called, as we have seen, design of the "offering" or offering design (offering-target set). This is a concept superior to that of product or a range of products and includes the vision of the client. It is not about doing something better or more beautifully, but about really understanding what the market wants. Once designed, the tactic will be responsible for shaping it, but if we have made a mistake in the design of the offering, tactics will not fix it.

When designing the offering, we observed that all of the strategy's components are simultaneously present. This is not a truly sequential process. When we innovate, we have to keep in mind the purpose of innovation, the perception of the client, what they want from us and how we position ourselves in the client's mental positioning map. It is not up to us to place ourselves where we want to be or where we think we are, but to understand how the client sees us in the market. Innovation is to succeed in the market. For Schumpeter the innovator is the entrepreneur who has a commercial vision, not the inventor of products. Steve Jobs was the innovator although he did not know anything about technology. Stephen Wozniak was the inventor, the super technologist, the one who was capable of manufacturing and designing which, in the first instance had been visualized by Jobs; he was not the innovator in the Schumpeterian sense of the word.

Therefore, in this phase of strategic design of the offering, we must simultaneously take into account the product and service that we want to design, the potential segments to provide it with sufficient differentiation, the competitors and our situation on the positioning map.

The potential segments will normally present complexity since they will be industrial and consumer segments belonging to different industries.

There is a wide range of resources explaining how to perform segmentation exercises. It is not the objective of this book to enter into this in detail although we could begin by generating a list of criteria to align the needs of the segments with the capabilities of the company in order to select target industries. Subsequently, it would be necessary to select the needs and desires of the customers (industrial and consumer) with our capabilities to generate the offer. In this way the offer could be generated in detail and even develop the capabilities that the company needs to meet the potential demand.

The criteria for segmentation will respond generically to the questions **WHAT, WHO, HOW, WHERE and WHEN**, in addition to the estimation of the size of the market. Answering these questions will produce a great generation of ideas and identification of opportunities as we will see later with an example.

The final result is that we will obtain a set of MMIX to apply to the selected segments. The MMIX generated, by definition, will be different. We could make the following classification:

- One MMIX for the entire market: Mass Market
- A different MMIX for each segment: Differentiation
- An equal MMIX for several segments: Undifferentiated market
- One MMIX for a single segment: Niche market

It is important to understand this classification. We could have a single MMIX for several segments due to the high manufacturing costs of many product lines, communication or other problems. We must be aware of what we do and how we can improve, always from the customer's point of view, avoiding sales to massive markets for simple comfort or lack of planning.

This can be illustrated as follows: we have mentioned previously that ideas usually occur to us as an offering-target set and that this is positive since it is the centre of the strategy. Although to be honest, in practice, much more weight falls on the offering than on the target. Usually we let ourselves get dragged along by our point of view (criterion of the own reference) and that is reflected in the offering instead of in the point of view of the client, the target.

This is true for many reasons. The first is that ideas occur to us, so it is natural that we develop them as we want. The second is that asking about or investigating the targets wants is tedious and complicated. The third is that, often we mistakenly think that our product is going to be liked by the whole world (mass market). The fourth one, (this only works for the visionaries) is that they know more than their clients and if they do something great they will succeed. This last reason was wielded by Steve Jobs and is reflected in some marketing books, in which it is argued that asking the market about new products does not usually provide quality information, since the market does not know yet. However, Steve Jobs was a genius; the rest of us will continue to consult the market.

An illustrative example is that of the electric car. This is an OFFERING type concept, it has to be given a good deal of form and definition before converting it into a product. But these decisions have to be made now, while it is still OFFERING. Once it becomes a product, we will not be able to do anything other than make tactical modifications.

Electric cars do not have a big market yet. The apparent reason is that they are expensive and have little autonomy. Spending € 35,000 on a car that can travel 250 km, when I have diesel substitute for € 20,000 that travels 1,000 km does not seem like a good option. There is however an electric car that is having particular success. This one costs € 90,000, from the Tesla brand, and covers 500 km. What is the reason for the success of the most expensive car? It lies in the design of the offering-target set. The € 90,000 Tesla is a bargain for quality and performance for the high-class buyer (target) who was going to buy an exclusive € 120,000 car.

Once the offering-target set is designed and made into a product, we can only continue with tactical decisions. These decisions will refer to aspects such as materials, colour, upholstery, guarantees or versions, but we can no longer change our strategic design offering / target. For this we will have to redesign, which will cost us time and money or something even more complex; we will be forced to modify our positioning because if we have decided to manufacture a car that the market does not want, the market will recognize us as -**the manufacturer of products that nobody wants.** In the meantime, we will lose money, our image and market share.

Doing a good job with the design of the offering-target set is fundamental, and we will refer to it when talking about the term COMPETITIVE ADVANTAGE, in the corresponding chapter.

11.6 PRACTICAL EXAMPLE

Segmentation is an exercise that is hard to carry out. We will develop an example with a sufficient level of detail to serve as a practical guide. The methodology is simple but effective at the same time.

Imagine that we are a recently formed company dedicated to receptive tourism. This business aims to give special treatment to small groups of tourists who arrive at a certain location.

Let's recall that the goal of segmentation is to solve the problem of the undifferentiated market, that is, to avoid offering our product to all customers in an undifferentiated way. This is the easiest and even the cheapest step, but also what works the worst. Giving each group of customers (segment) a differentiated product works better, although it also makes production, activities and management more expensive. The micro-segmentation or determination of the individual segment (each person) would be ideal, but often it is not feasible. We have to look for the midpoint and select the targets that are most convenient for us.

We could be tempted to open a web page welcoming all types of tourists but things do not work well like that. We will begin then by doing the easiest thing, which is to analyse our offering. The city on which the company is based is by the seaside, as well as offering the possibility of mountain excursions; it has a range of good restaurants and gastronomy, some golf courses and a rich cultural heritage. These five characteristics can serve as a basis to structure our offer and feedback the design phase of the offering (which tries to respond to 'the WHAT').

Once we have the offer we may continue to think "Why limit ourselves? Let's make it available to everyone!"

This is not a good idea. Although it is counter intuitive, making our offer available to everyone goes against the concept of segmentation. This would be like the difference between hunting and fishing. When we fish, we passively wait to see what goes in; when we hunt, we actively go for it. Remember that marketing actions require time and money. We will look for the most compatible clients, easy to reach, with economic capacity or other criteria that interest us.

The word criteria is revealing. What criteria should we consider to define our segments? This is a great challenge and one of the keys to the success of the strategy we are generating. Remember that the criteria must respond generically to the questions WHAT, WHO, HOW, WHERE and WHEN.

Some criteria that we can consider for this particular business could be the ease of access to the city, economic capacity and size of the market. Which clients comply with these three concepts? They could meet customers who live in large, nearby cities. In large cities it will be easier to find customers with economic capacity (WHO).

Which cities? These cities may be those that have a direct flight from the airport of our location. In our particular case these cities are London, Frankfurt, Paris and Madrid. Additionally, we can think of two smaller cities that are less than three hours away by bus and that we will call them C1 and C2 (WHERE).

We can present the results in a table. We see that the combination of five offerings against six segments already gives us thirty possible targets for which we must develop their respective MMIX (guides, communication in different languages, specific content, the HOW). This is already a significant amount of work. We restrict the market and generate more work! But the results will be worth it.

TARGET / OFFERING	LONDON	FRANKFURT	PARIS	MADRID	C1	C2
GOLF						
CITY TOUR						
GASTRO						
SEA						
MOUNTAIN						

Let's recall that the goal of segmentation is to better serve a subset of the market. Since our company is starting its activities and we do not have resources for everything, we will select the targets indicated in the table. Later we will expand to other targets as we have more availability of resources.

TARGET / OFFERING	LONDON	FRANKFURT	PARIS	MADRID	C1	C2
GOLF						
CITY TOUR	Target 1			Target 2		
GASTRO	Target 3			Target 4		
SEA						
MOUNTAIN						

We chose these targets because we consider that they offer a balance between ease and profitability. Starting activities in several languages can be complicated. Doing it first in English and Spanish is easier. At the same time, the city tours and the gastronomic offers are the easiest to implement, they do not require complicated negotiations with suppliers and they are both carried out within the cities, simplifying the logistics.

Once this first phase of the segmentation is finished, we will proceed to the second phase, which consists of studying the selected target in detail, trying to find out some key points. These key points are:

- WHAT the customer wants (the famous ´WHAT´, in detail)
- Your decision process
- The factors that influence you in the decision process

We do this to better outline our offer and establish a business model that facilitates communication with the client in their decision-making process. Note that this phrase contains three aspects of the strategy found in the MSSM®. The design of our offer and the business model form the basis of differentiation. Communication with the client, understanding where the points of influence are, is the culmination of the strategy.

To do this in a practical way you can follow the following process. Write three blocks with the following information:

First block:

1. Name your significant target

2. Describe the target, who is the client, what are its WHAT´s main attributes

3. Identify who makes the decision

4. Try to identify WHAT that target wants, what it values, what it prioritizes, in as much detail as you can.

Second block:

1. Draw, from top to bottom and in sequence, the customer's decision-making process or purchasing behaviour.

Third block:

1. Identify factors that influence the client in each sequence of the decision-making process (the second block).

Once this process is completed you will have a deeper knowledge of your customer's purchasing behaviour and you will be able to take the necessary actions to satisfy it.

We will do the example with Target 1 and 3, London customers who want City Tours and Gastronomic Offerings.

First block:

1. Name: British oriented culture & gastronomic tour.

2. Description of the Target:

This point of identification of the target is usually complicated to perform. Normally we tend to simplify it by focusing in on age group and gender and, paradoxically, covering all existing groups thus destroying once again the purpose of segmentation. For example, to say that the target is made up of men and women between the ages of 20 and 80 is to say nothing at all. We must avoid this by focusing on the information that is really relevant and useful in order to to then configure the offer and make marketing decisions. The purpose of this work is to be able to then take specific actions, both in the design of the offering and in the tactical implementation.

Let's try to specify a little more in the description. Categorization could be as follows:

- young couples (YC)
- senior retired couples (SRC)
- groups of young friends (GYF)
- groups of retired friends (GRF)
- Professional groups and companies (PG)

This way of categorizing allows us to go a little deeper into the customer's knowledge. From the outset we have sub-segmented the market in the consumer market and the professional (WHO), identifying the fact that that there may be companies interested in our services. In almost all cases of segmentation we will find a consumer market and a corporate one. We also observe the difference between young clients and retirees. Besides wanting different things, they will come at different periods of time (WHEN). Young people will come in summer and on weekends. Retirees and companies may also come during the week.

We will represent the results in the table, but to simplify, we will only deal with the clients in London.

TARGET OFFERING	LONDON				
CITY TOUR	YC	SRC	GYF	GRF	PG
GASTRO	YC	SRC	GYF	GRF	PG

3. Who makes the decision?

The purchase decision will be taken up differently by different groups and this will help us to design the communication strategy with the client. In the case of professionals and companies, the decisions will be taken by those responsible for marketing, purchasing or human resources when planning their company's events. We will have to analyse this in detail.

With regard to couples or groups, it is necessary to understand what criteria are used. For example, a possible scenario could be identified that it is the woman who decides based on criteria of security, trust and specific quality of the offering (or the other way around).

According to the findings, the offering would be adapted to the needs or requirements of the person making the final decision.

4. What does the client want?

Obviously this is the most difficult question. The answer will be almost always incomplete, but the mere fact of trying to answer it will give us a lot of information.

The YC and GYF targets may require offers based on fun, trendy or emblematic places, visits related to sports events, with more activity and more freedom, while SRC and GRF may want quieter places, less activity, more cultural and more controlled. PG on the other hand could require the inclusion of a business session or similar.

With this information, we would be in a position to structure the offer for each target. In our concrete case we could join YC with GYF and SRC with GRF since they are sufficiently related in order to simplify the actions. We would therefore have six targets (within LONDON), which we could call YO, RE, PG.

TARGET OFFERING	LONDON		
CITY TOUR	YO	RE	PG
GASTRO	YO	RE	PG

We will continue the analysis with the second block.

Second block:

1. Draw, from top to bottom and in sequence, the decision making process of the client, the purchasing behaviour.

This procedure is similar to the one known as Journey Map (look it up on the internet), which reflects the steps a customer takes to complete a purchase process and how he or she interacts with collaborators and suppliers. This process aims to identify, simulating a real case, the needs that are presented and the options to satisfy them.

To perform this exercise we will select a target, although we would have to do it with everyone. We can select the RE target.

What is the process that a retiree follows to choose a mini break? We can contrast it with what we do ourselves (instead of drawing it we will use a list).

a) Search for information
b) Ask friends or other users
c) Search suppliers
d) Preselect offers
e) Compare prices and benefits
f) Contact supplier
g) Specify details and price
h) Hire and pay

Consider whether or not this is a valid model. Propose ideas or variants. We will complete this information with the third block.

Third block:

1. Identify factors that influence the client in each sequence of the decision-making process.

The purchase process identified in the previous step must be completed identifying the factors that influence the customer. These factors will be strongly linked to the concepts of differentiation that we identified at the time. These are: design of the offering, business model, processes that support it and communication or customer perception.

a. Search for information:

1. Where are you looking for information? List sources. Do retirees surf the internet? Are there specific websites in your country? Are there specific channels? Are there local providers? Are there magazines, publications, clubs or associations of retirees?

2. Do the airlines themselves communicate the possible

offers? Do airports do it?

3. Are there specific travel agencies for retirees?

b. Ask friends or other users.

How are they referenced? Can you create a database of reference and experiences? External references?

c. Search for a provider.

Do we respond to the client's WHAT? Can the customer find us, see us?

d. Pre-select Offers.

Do we comply with the minimum standards?

e. Compare Price and benefits

Are we moving within a range desired by our targets?

f. Contact the provider

Is it easy to contact? Do they require phoning? Is it convenient enough?

g. Specify details and price

Is it easily configurable by the user? Does the client abandon the page or not? Do we transmit confidence?

h. Hire and pay

Do we have sufficient means of payment for the client to accept? Is the process simple?

This process should provide us with the information we need so that at least, on paper, our offering, business model and process design, are perceived positively by the client. From here we can identify the points of improvement in our offering, what we lack or what we can improve. This is a point of direct application for the Blue Ocean theory (W. Chan Kim, R. Mauborgne: Blue Ocean Strategy). What can we create that does not exist? What can we improve? What can we eliminate from what exists? What can we reduce?

The segmentation process, so often forgotten about, is the central point of the strategy. It allows us to combine multiple related concepts related and extract important conclusions of immediate application.

At the end of this process we will obtain the matrix to which we have referred as a directional matrix or GE matrix. In rows we will have our set of offerings in order of priority. In columns we will have the set of chosen segments, or targets. This matrix, once identified, must be kept alive and kicking. We will continue to generate offerings as a result of our innovation process, which we will put on the market in due time. We will continue to identify new segments to serve.

Additionally, we will have a descriptive sheet of each target, which we will also keep alive, with all the relevant information about each of the segments studied.

11.7 WHAT IS SWOT USED FOR?

SWOT is a tool widely used as a basis to structure brainstorming sessions. These sessions, in turn, aim to identify or assess the state of a situation in relation to the four components of the SWOT, which as everyone knows, are the Weaknesses, Threats, Strengths and Opportunities. According to the results of the session, those participating have data on which to base further decision making.

All this is very good but in practice we have two problems that make this tool of very little value.

The first problem is that the SWOT sessions are not prepared. Normally we are summoned to a meeting to which we go, I insist, without any preparation and in which we are encouraged to say anything we can think of to generate ideas. Sometimes even participants from outside the industry are invited to achieve "cross-pollination", that is, ideas from other industries (one of the components of the theory of innovation) to apply them to ours. The result is usually a pot pourri of random thoughts instead of genuine ideas.

In order to develop a SWOT, a complete situational analysis must be carried out first. The data resulting from the analysis is the input data of the SWOT. When performing a SWOT you do not have to invent anything that particular morning but you have to go with the data well prepared and even converted into information (the data will be included in the template provided in chapter nine).

Obviously, to convert data into information, one must have industrial knowledge of the sector that we are analysing. That is why the participants in a SWOT exercise must be knowledgeable experts in the industry, with years of experience. Evidently, participation can be opened up to people from outside the industry or with less experience in order to provide other points of view and certain freshness to the session, but the foundations have to be solid.

The second problem is that the SWOT is usually left unfinished. When we consider that we have already filled in the four quadrants identifying their components, the team feels satisfied and finishes the exercise.

This is an error. The SWOT is an exercise used to consolidate data from the situational analysis and prepare it for the next phase, that of generating a solid strategy. To do this, it is necessary to extract information from the SWOT.

The methodology tells us that the SWOT has two quadrants belonging to the outside world, threats and opportunities, which are common to all companies competing in that market. From these two quadrants, the so-called Critical Success Factors are extracted or in other words, what the market requires. In order to simplify, we will call this the WHAT, what the market wants (the WHAT already identified in the segmentation).

The other two quadrants, strengths and weaknesses refer only to our company. From his point it is necessary to extract what is known as Distinctive Capabilities of the company, or in other words, how we satisfy the WHAT of the market. For simplicity, we will call this the HOW (the HOW already identified in the design of the offering).

We can already see that the WHAT has a lot of information stemming from the exercise of segmentation and targeting, one of the most important exercises in the analysis, while the HOW has a lot of information stemming from the process of innovation, differentiation, capacity of design of the offering, processes of the company and business models.

All this does not end here. As we have already seen, our offering and the customer's needs are closely linked concepts that do not exist in isolation. The WHAT and the HOW have to match. If they do, our OFFERING-TARGET set will have, at least on paper, a competitive advantage and we will continue working to increase this. Nevertheless, we must work to increase our strengths and detect new opportunities.

If all this is carried out in this fashion, the SWOT will be an important productivity tool. Failing that, it will be of little worth.

To ensure that we are actually using the SWOT as a data consolidation tool in a procedural manner, we will audit the competitive advantage of our offering. The process is detailed in the next chapter.

SWOT and competitive advantage

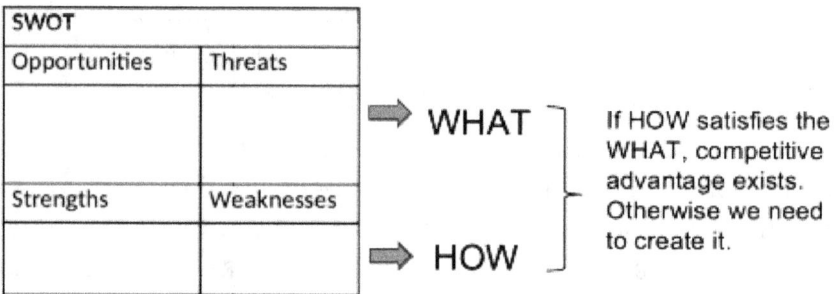

11.8 COMPETITIVE ADVANTAGE

Following on from this phase of analysis we must be able to extract from the SWOT the WHAT and the HOW as we have previously seen. It seems easy but experience tells me that when I ask which five factors are the most important to your client, answers will not come easily and are often too general or obvious. If we do not have clarity on this point, how are we going to create a successful offering?

The processes that we have seen previously should allow us to understand the WHAT in sufficient detail since they incorporate the wishes, needs and requirements of our client and the associated market; this includes concepts related to perception, such as a commercial brand, those who must be satisfied by our HOW, the offering of the company specially designed for that target. Here, the capacities and potentialities of our company are gathered together to create the offering.

If the WHAT and the HOW match we can say that we have a competitive advantage for this OFFERING / TARGET. We will propose a suitable methodology to audit our competitive advantage in order to find out if we have cracked it or not. In this way the concept will transition from being abstract to tangible and you as a strategist will be able to squeeze it to the maximum.

It is interesting to note that this exercise will be done by OFFERING / TARGET since analysing the competitive advantage of, for example, an entire company, is too diffuse. However, it could also be applied at the corporate level and sometimes it will be necessary to do so.

To define the competitive advantage we will use three concepts. The first is to meet market requirements, the second is to do this with sufficient differentiation and the third evaluates whether this differentiation is sustainable over time. They are synthetic concepts but they incorporate a lot of information. The first concept summarizes the information of the customer segmentation process and the design of the offering. The second summarizes the information of the offering and the competitors since the differentiation is compared between them. The third reflects our capacity for innovation since we can only maintain our differentiation if we are innovative: company, offering and targets, competitors and innovation. We have all the components of the strategy summarized in a table.

To represent it visually we will rely on a tool known as Quality Function Deployment or QFD matrix, developed by Yoji Akao and used in companies such as Toyota and Mitsubishi. This matrix, also called the House of Quality due its visual aspect and purpose, has been used widely in manufacturing processes to ensure that the requirements of a phase of production are satisfied by the previous one in order to avoid errors when possible. You can see multiple examples of this matrix on the internet.

Here we will use a simplified adaptation of this. We will create a table in which, the rows will be the requirements of the clients and the market, the WHAT, arranged in order of priority, the columns will represent, the HOW, or our way of satisfying them. Within each box we will write the three concepts previously defined as constituents of the competitive advantage. We will put a Y for yes or an N for no, depending on the answer to each question. In the second question, if we do not have enough differentiation, we will put the name of our competitor or an N. In this way, at a glance we can see a revealing amount of information in a very synthetic way.

This tool does not produce a yes / no result, but allows us to evaluate, individually or in a working group, our level of competitive advantage as well as identify areas for improvement. The competitive advantage is the product of our strategy and through this procedure we establish a control point in order to recognize it. Depending on the result we will continue with the process or we will go back to the drawing board to redesign.

Let's take a look all this with a practical example. We will continue with the case seen in the segmentation and in particular with the RE target. The first question is, as we already know, what our target wants. We will choose only six factors, although you have to put all those that are relevant to you, sorted by priority.

1. Simple and easy website & telephone access in English: ACCESS
2. Trust and ease of payment & possibility of cancellations: PAYMENT
3. Airport transportation: AIRPORT
4. Quality cultural offer, museum, event, tour: CULTURE
5. All-inclusive gastronomic offer: GASTRO
6. Luxury hotel: LUXURY

The second step is to check if we satisfy those factors. To do this, let's build the table (matrix QFD).

Audit of the Competitive Advantage

Identify the Competitive Advantage. If you are not able to do it, you do not have it yet. If you have difficulty doing this exercise, you need to acquire more knowledge of your industry.

Do it by offering / target or unit of analysis.

WHAT does my client want	Priority	HOW do we satisfy this (components of our offering)				
		Supportive Technology Design	Transport included	Local offer agreements	Local offer	5 stars
Access	1	YYY				
Payment	2	YYY				
Airport	3		YNN			
Culture	4			YNN		
Gastro	5				YNN	
Luxury	6					YNN

At a glance we can appreciate that we do not have a clear competitive advantage. In other words, our competitors can offer basically the same as we offer, since the basic product, the cultural offer, the gastronomy and the accommodation are available to all competitors.

We can only create differentiation with the services around the base product, that is, the associated services, the processes and the business model (we will return later to this concept in Tactics). In our case we have an access service designed in a differentiated way that allows you to navigate easily, configure an offer that is appropriate to the customer's wishes, access telephone support, pay easily and retract if necessary. If this is not provided by the competition because it requires an effort in the design, we will have an advantage there. Nevertheless, this does not seem sufficient.

In this case, we will have to continue working to create a differentiated offer through additional services to the base services. Starting a business with a negative diagnosis of competitive advantage is a mistake we can avoid. Note that when we consider this analysis, the simple identification of WHAT has already become a problem. I have often seen the board of directors of a company hesitate or stop to think when asked what customers want or what they value. This is a question that we have to ask continuously, and find the answers, although the response will change over time.

When completing the picture, it is normal to find diagonal information. It is not necessary to fill in all the boxes, only where applicable. The diagonal will be complete, along with another box.

Sometimes it may be that we get a clear competitive advantage in all the boxes except one which is so strong as to neutralize the entire offering. This is what is called a **Limiting Factor**, a single factor that makes the project impossible. This is clearly seen in the case of Audi versus Citroën. A Citroën C6 may be better than an Audi A6, but the brand, affordable versus luxury, is a limiting factor that neutralizes the other advantages of the model in question.

Remember that when the concept of Competitive Advantage was generated, it was identified as something essential to stand out in the market, be a leader and better than the rest. Nowadays, in order to survive, it is considered as an essential element necessary simply to be in the market. Consequentially, we can appreciate the importance of establishing a process that allows us to monitor this.

11.9 POSITIONING

We will dedicate a whole chapter to positioning due to the importance that it has. Normally the concepts of segmentation, targeting and positioning go together in the description of the marketing strategy. We have considered this in the previous chapter, although we will develop some additional concepts here.

As we have previously seen, positioning is the point where we are in touch with the mental, perceptual map of the client. It is very important in marketing to truly distinguish client perception from tangible facts. Which is the more important of the two? Whether you like it or not, or you find this difficult to accept, it is in actual fact the perception.

History is full of examples of very good products that failed against other worse ones. There have also been the cases of excellent standards that were replaced by others which were by far inferior as has been seen so many times in the computer industry. Indeed whole industries that have been created around products do not perform well as is the case of planned obsolescence. There are also many useless products, that border on fraudulent but that sell well.

Some nascent industries, such as free software, require you to dedicate a part of your effort in order to adapt it and maintain it against your own opportunity cost (and therefore your profitability). Even so, the market accepts them, so it is to be assumed that there are reasons for this even if they are not exclusively based on efficiency and performance.

It is therefore a matter of understanding these reasons or of making our own reasons visible. We will work on these two points well to adapt our product to the needs and desires of the client or to adapt our client to our needs and desires, respectively. The first is done through the design of the offering. The second is done through the communication plan. Therefore, the communication plan is of strategic importance for the company and is often referred to as a strategic communication plan.

The communication plan is so important that it has its own SOSTAC® whose tactic is the media plan. If the client does not see us with their eyes on his or her personal mental map of positioning, our strategy does not exist or does not work. It's that simple. If we do not exist for the client (or for the channel) quite simply, we do not exist. We have a strategic error that must be corrected alongside the design of the offering. Sometimes, if our product or service is really well designed, it can simply be corrected by working on the communication plan. A case like this happened to the well-known Guinness company. Young consumers did not drink black beer (they did not see it) and the market therefore went down gradually over the years. They had to design a strategic communications plan to position the brand again in the minds of consumers. This is an example in which you can see the power of communication and the perception of the product.

The same can be said of some generalist car manufacturers whose high-end models do not manage to compete with the saloon cars established at that point of the positioning map. Returning to an example that we have already discussed, a Citroen C6 cannot compete against an Audi A6 (I will not enter into assessing which car is better). However, no matter how good the car is, this does not position a manufacturer that has small and cheap cars in the same way as another one that only has large, and some small but expensive cars. This is what Toyota and Nissan have understood by creating their own brand of expensive cars, Lexus and Infinity. This is based quite simply on customer perception.

A positioning map is usually represented by two variables in order to simplify. The easiest is usually quality versus price, although any dimension can be represented. Below you can see how the company, Marketing for SMEs (M4P) positions its offering in the market.

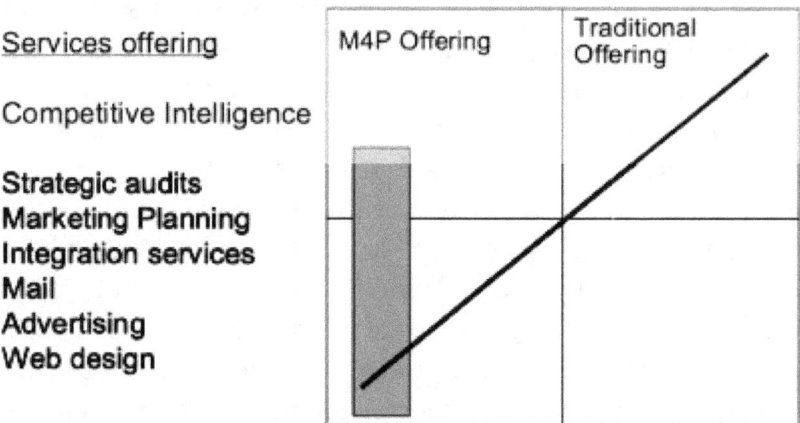

M4P Positioning Decision

Positioning of M4P

In this table you can see how the traditional marketing services offer increases in tune with the increase of the budget capacity of the client, leaving an unattended market corresponding to small businesses. The company M4P is positioned to serve this market by providing services that cover most of the needs for clients with lower economic capacity. The objective is to visualize what place we occupy in relation to our competitors and how to reflect on what we offer in order to differentiate ourselves from them. We will therefore occupy that position in the market, but we must ensure that customers see us in the aforementioned position.

It's interesting to consider what Intel did in order to get customers to see the company with their own eyes; quite a challenge for a microprocessor locked in a case inside a computer. Few people would be willing to respond to the question, "What does a microprocessor do?" The same applies if you were to ask how many types or manufacturers, or models, or processor speeds there are. Nevertheless if you were going to buy a computer and it does not have the "Intel inside" sticker, you may not buy it. Why? You do not know the reason (sorry for being so blunt), but perception works like that. Intel knew this.

That's why communication is strategic. But also, you have to sell the meaning of the strategy. The design of our offering has to have strategic content. This will allow us to position ourselves high on the client's mental perception map. But what is selling strategy?

We sell strategy when our offer is adapted and overlaps the value chain of our client, when their needs of higher value are satisfied by our offering in a differentiated way. Therefore, it is important to identify areas of high customer value. What is it that the client really needs or wants? The higher we are able to ascend in the value chain of the client, the better we can design the offering, the higher the prices and margins and the higher quality will be reflected in the level of dialogue we have with our client. Let's go back to an example that we have already discussed, Seiko sells watches, while Rolex sells jewellery. They have positioned themselves in very different places within the range of market options. This is the strategic content that leads to positioning.

Obviously this is easy to say, the difficult thing is to put it into practice; to do so identification is key. When you set your goals, go the extra mile to make them as strategic as possible.

Do a gap analysis of your company (as we saw in chapter 8). This is done by evaluating where you are and establishing where you want to go. Set goals to get there. Evaluate your objectives and separate them into strategic and tactical ones. What's the score? This will help you to define a little better the design of your strategy. If for example you have a restaurant, improving the ingredients of the daily menu is a tactical goal, but launching a new home delivery service is a strategic one.

Now you are in a position to discern a little more methodically which objectives and actions are strategic and which are tactics.

Some strategic actions could be:

- Balance of the product portfolio
- Adapt resources with business needs
- Evaluation of competitive advantage
- Identify customer needs
- Neutralize competitors' strengths
- Implement innovation process
- Moving up the client's value chain
- Design communication content
- Reposition the company or offering

Some tactical actions could be:

- Creation of an autonomous website
- Specific advertising campaign
- Promotional pricing
- Product line restructuring
- Encourage sales force
- Negotiation of prices with the channel
- Product technical improvement
- Improvement of product image

Each component of the tactics, of the 7 Ps, has a strategic aspect that must be defined in the strategic phase. The design of the product within the offering is strategic but then, its details are tactical. The price decision is strategic when it contributes to positioning the product, the brand or the company, although its subsequent variations are tactical. Logically, once a decision has been established for the creation and positioning of a product, it will be very difficult to modify it, so this decision is strategic.

If for example, we decide to create an expensive product and position it as such, we cannot then change the price or vice versa, unless you do it through a very complex repositioning project. If you create a brand of expensive watches or cars and for some reason you are forced to lower the price, you lose the premium product positioning and it will be almost impossible to recover it.

Negotiation with the correct channels can be strategic if it gives us certain advantages of exclusivity, entry into new markets or access to certain clients. It will be tactical if it refers to temporary changes or no added value. Communication will be strategic when it is part of the design of the offering but it will be tactical if it only responds to the generation of discretionary campaigns.

The positioning of a company in the market therefore is twofold. One is to define where we want to be, where we want our strategy design to be placed in the market; this must be included within the company's objectives. The second consideration is to make sure that the desired positioning is actually seen by the client; this will be accomplished by strategic communication.

11.10 STRATEGIC COMMUNICATION

Communication is such an important concept in marketing that all too often identifies bi-univocally albeit incorrectly.

Normally, companies spend a lot of time developing the communication plan, the media plan or on negotiations with the companies that develop these for them.

Here we could also differentiate what kind of activity belongs to the tactics of communication and which to the strategic one. The communication plan is so important that it has its own SOSTAC® plan, parallel to the business plan and included in it. Within the communication plan, the tactic, which used to be the 7 Ps, is now composed of the media plan, that is, in which media we will carry out the communication actions, with its associated detail.

Where is the communication strategy then? The communication strategy consists of identifying accurately the elements of differentiation that we are going to communicate to our target and making sure that the target actually sees us.

Quite simply if clients do not see us, or do not see what we want them to see (our positioning), we will have failed. We may well have the rest of the strategy well developed, but the client does not see this and therefore does not buy from us. The strategy is broken by the weakest point and fails.

That is why before developing our communication campaigns (tactics) we design a solid strategy. The writer Simon Sinek explains and develops the concept of 'WHY', in addition to the 'WHAT' and the 'HOW', to convey our differentiation to the client.

https://www.ted.com/talks/simon_sinek_how_great_leaders_inspire_action

This exercise of thinking about what we want to communicate is very useful and produces feedback. It is not always easy to generate differentiating proposals. Actually it is very difficult. Think constantly about what your client wants, how you could improve what you currently have. Communicate with the client in a way that he or she hears what they want to hear (the ´WHY¨) instead of the requirements of the design (the ´WHAT¨) or our means of achieving it (the ´HOW´).

We will be talking about the same thing, but we are communicating it in a different way. When you carry out this process, ideas will emerge that you should take advantage of in order to incorporate them in a real way into your product or services, increasing their differentiation. The exercise of communicating your offering to the client allows you to visualize what the client would like and thus improve your offer.

I have many examples that illustrate this fact. We have already mentioned the Intel case. Intel has made it its business to be seen, literally by the clients' eyes. This no longer depends on the intermediaries since ultimately the customer sees it and asks for it. They had to create that masterful strategy since the processor, by itself, is impossible to see by the normal user. There are other manufacturers, but you do not see them. They may have a good strategy, but you do not see it. The same goes for Microsoft with its Xbox. From a young age, children know the company and associate it with something fun. Then, incrementally, this vision reaches the professional and business environment.

You have to communicate your strategy to the client, your ´WHY´, your enthusiasm, your reason for doing things. Communicating the strategy increases the level of conversation and dialogue with your client. The client will think about you more and will ask you in advance; thus the relationship will be more advisory (strategic) than operational (tactical) and less dependent on the price. Remember that the price is established on the basis of differentiation and that it must be seen and understood by your client.

A little emotion will always be well received, because emotion is the currency of life. In fact, it could be said that the emotional component is the predominant one in decision making. As absurd as it seems many decisions are poor in rationale and very emotional (sometimes even dependent on the hormonal situation of each). Buying a top of the range SUV that will never go through the mud is an emotional purchase; buying a 600 euro mobile phone is too. Observe this fact and try to accommodate it within your strategy. Often we try to impose reason in our arguments when really this has absolutely no sense because the decision is not going to be rational but emotional. You must try to understand the emotional requirements of your client. This is what strategic communication is based on. No matter how good your product is, if this fails, the entire chain will fail, the entire strategic process will fail. It does not matter if you're right or not. We tend to give too much importance to the value of our proposals but the value, obviously, is already assumed to be included. On the other hand, we do not give importance to emotional contact with our clients. Without this emotional contact we are lost and not everyone is aware of the importance of this point. The entire company must transmit and communicate emotion.

Let's go back to the case of Citroën. Citroën has had to reformulate its strategic communication (neither its tactics, nor its products) and create a brand of luxury cars, DS, to position itself in that market and make itself visible to its customers. The products, except in their design, will not be very different; the communication tactics will not be either. However, the deep concept of strategic communication, of emotion, has had to be modified. Action such as this has already been taken in the past by other manufacturers, such as the aforementioned cases of Toyota creating Lexus or Nissan creating Infinity.

A short time ago in a marketing seminar, one of the students asked me the following about a company, "where is that company, which is no longer seen?" The question came in handy for introduction of this subject. The curious thing is that the company to which he was referring was not being seen by the student due to a strategic decision made by the management to withdraw from a certain segment of the consumer market. Of course, the company was seen by its corresponding targets. This reflects a correct definition and implementation of the marketing strategy.

In short, our target has to see the result of our strategy. If this is correct, we must develop the most effective media plan for our purposes, communication tactics. However, a correct tactic will not be effective on an incorrect design of communication strategy, as the case of Citroën shows. No matter how good the product or the media plan is, the client will not see us and will not buy from us.

Remember, identify the WHAT of the client and build your HOW. When you talk to your clients, tell them about the WHY. People do not like to be told what they need to be doing, or to hear explanations about what is happening to them; the client does not want your lessons; they prefer to listen to the reasons why a company creates products and services in a differentiating way which gives them enjoyment.

As the great philosopher Nietzsche said, `He who has a why to live can bear almost any how'. The one who discovers the "why" that motivates his clients will find the "how" to reach them (Thanks to Nietzsche for his kind permission to share this).

Over the years I have seen how many companies, even with good products, ignored the market's perception of them. They were simply not interested in knowing. The way in which the client sees you is the final result of your strategy and it is something that must always be monitored. Furthermore, clients are a great source for new ideas.

11.11 RECAPITULATION

Strategy is a process that culminates with the creation of competitive advantage for the company. The next time someone asks you what your company's strategy or competitive advantage is, your response as a strategist will be to tell them that you will need at least one hour to respond as there are several relevant aspects that need to be explained in detail.

Strategy has six aspects that must be addressed simultaneously. The first is the innovation process, which must be implemented and be recognizable in the company. This process is what allows ideas to be generated; the more there are and the greater the variety the better. The process must be based on training, knowledge and analysis. It is innovation that will generate ideas to fuel differentiation.

Differentiation is the second aspect and is the central component of competitive advantage. Differentiation is already linked from the beginning to the third aspect, which is that of the offering.

When we think of differentiating ourselves, we think of a product or service and a context of customers and competitors, although differentiation can in turn be applied to any element of the company or to the dimensions of the product (increased product) such as the after-sales service, the delivery terms or any other attribute including the business model. Differentiation may continue to develop later during the implementation of any of the 7 Ps.

The fourth aspect is the target, which is obtained through the segmentation process. This allows us to refine the design of the differentiating components adapting them better to the needs of the clients and making us strive towards a deeper understanding of those needs (offering-target set).

The fifth aspect is positioning, which is the culmination of the entire process and the place where our offering is located slap bang in the middle of the clients' field of vision. If the client does not see us, something has gone wrong or has not worked.

Strategic communication, the sixth aspect, ensures that the target customers see us (perceive us) in their mental map of positioning. What Toyota did with its new Prius is strategic communication. It has gone up on the positioning map with a better and more expensive car with a somewhat "strange" design (by using the term strange I avoid the problem of using another adjective). Why did Toyota make such a daring design? The answer is in order to differentiate itself and avoid customers comparing it with an Audi or something similar. The buyer of a new Prius is not going to make many comparisons because the product is so different to others; this creates leadership and loyalty in the market.

If we have accomplished all our tasks well, our company will have a competitive advantage, that is, it will have different types of customers (segments, targets) whose needs (the WHAT) will be identified and satisfied in a differentiated way by our offerings, (the HOW) and whose differentiation will be good enough to stand up to its competitors and be perceived as such (the WHY) to remain in the market in a sustainable manner at least in the medium term.

11.12 PRICE AND DIFFERENTIATION

I do not usually like to talk about price. So often we are tempted to say that our product will have an adjusted price so that it sells well. But the price can be calculated in a precise way. There is a price that is mathematically optimal so that the margin multiplied by the volume gives us the maximum benefit. This price can be defined very easily; it only depends on two variables. The optimal price is the maximum price someone would pay for our product plus the variable costs, all divided by two. It would be the technically called price of elasticity equal to one, if the variable costs were zero. This price, moreover, is independent of the slope of the demand line (the volume will not be). The calculations and some examples are developed in my book **Economy to Leave Home,** also for sale on Amazon.

That is to say, that the optimal price of our product is directly related to our old and strategic friend, DIFFERENTIATION. The maximum price someone would be willing to pay for our product depends on the differentiation we have and to what extent our client appreciates it. Obviously, if we do not have differentiation, the price will be that of our competitors. Competing for price is always something to avoid and a symptom of strategic drift.

Therefore, let's develop differentiation and calculate the optimal price that must be assigned. This will also give us new ideas about the reasoning of customers when valuing our products. Contrary to what we usually think intuitively, consumers like expensive and valuable goods, (not products without value offered at a high price). Look at the brands that are most successful and their prices. Usually they correspond to companies that are doing very well. In French, Italian or English, expensive means desired, loved, wanted, dear. We desire goods that are expensive, different, special and valuable.

The objective of an advanced society is to produce expensive goods with value: expensive energy because it does not pollute, expensive medicine, expensive high quality products, even high taxes, to pay for good government services, good education, a good health service, good pensions. The current fashion of cheapening everything by reducing quality is, in my view, an error (please, do not remove the co-pilot to reduce de price of airline tickets).

Creating expensive products and services is equivalent to saying that the society that produces them works hard and efficiently, generating value. Sometimes value can be placed in direct correspondence with the price. Let's take an example. My company develops a product that produces savings for customers who use it. The savings are X€ per year. The maximum price that a client would be willing to pay would therefore be X€ per year. From this point, as the price goes down, a net saving for the client begins to be produced. The more the savings, the more customers will be encouraged to buy my product.

Let's think that my product costs Y€ per year to produce and maintain, on an annualized basis. Then the optimal selling price, as we said before, is half of X+Y. Possibly you will already be wondering if you should consider this or that cost as fixed or variable, but this is actually a different ways of seeing the same thing.

Reducing variable costs is a clear objective since in doing so we earn twice as much. On the one hand we approach the point of elasticity equal to one, which allows us to sell more quantity. On the other hand, the contribution increases, that is, the difference between the sale price and the variable costs. We sell more and with more margin.

Therefore, reducing supply costs is something that must always be done, unless we want to deliberately increase them to produce something of more value that gives rise to another line of demand that positions us in another market. However, reducing costs has a limited journey. If we do it well, we will soon reach our destination.

We will consequently have to work on the other variable, differentiation. This variable, on the other hand, has no limit, is open to our imagination (supported by solid methodologies and industrial knowledge, obviously) and is the basis of our strategy. A solid strategy will allow high prices. Look around you at the companies that sell their products at high prices, as they tend to be those with the most loyal customers.

Once you have determined your reference price by means of the exposed calculation, you can dedicate your time and energy to making tactical variations in order to achieve certain objectives. The most widely used sources tells us that the process to establish a price is the following:

1. Identification of the demand line
2. Determination of the pricing strategy
3. Identification of costs and volumes
4. Identification of competitors' prices and costs
5. Adoption of a reference method
6. Price definition and contextual adjustments

We have avoided calculating the demand line using the concept of the maximum price. However, calculating it is always useful to obtain volumes and therefore theoretical benefits.

The pricing strategy refers to whether we want to increase volumes at the cost of lowering prices or vice versa (penetration, growth, collection of profits, transfer price) and depends on the type of market we are in, product life cycle and other concepts of this nature.

The identification of costs and volumes is necessary to verify if we move within the productive capacities of the company and how we position ourselves in terms of benefits when calculating the theoretical optimal price.

The prices and costs of the competitors will provide us with valuable information to help us understand where we stand on the positioning map.

The reference method refers to the use of the most common references such as margin on sales or on costs. It is interesting to note that establishing a reference method without first calculating a reference price based on the point of maximum benefit is an error. Deciding for example, that you are going to apply a 100% margin to the cost price without knowing how that decision places you in terms of theoretical expected profit, does not make sense. You have to do it the other way around, first calculate the optimum point and then verify the corresponding margin. It is also a mistake to include the fixed costs in the calculation since it will hide the identification of the optimal price.

Make your calculations, but first think of the concept of maximum price that a customer would pay for your product and therefore, what value it should incorporate. Prioritizing costs is an error although obviously we have to work to contain them, but taking care that the cost savings do not decrease the value of our offer (do not let yourself be carried away by the easy option, which is to make cheap goods, lacking in value).

The ideas of M. Porter recommend avoidance of competing with prices in order to avoid falling into the point called "stuck in the middle". This is when the item is not the cheapest and does not have the necessary value to differentiate. Although these ideas simple and well known, they are not sufficiently internalized or are manifestly difficult to carry out.

12 TACTICS. REINFORCING DIFFERENTIATION

What are tactics in a marketing plan? The tactic of marketing is made up of the well-known 4 Ps or 7 Ps when we also include services. It is very frequent to relate the word marketing with the Ps or even with just one of them, the P of promotions (communication) or furthermore, with one of the components of communication, advertising.

Therefore, the tactic is the definition in detail of the decisions made in the strategy that will become reality via the action plans. This detail is made up of the Product (or service), the Price, the sales channel (Place), the communication (Promotions), the Process (base of the business model), the professionals (People) and the physical evidence of the company (Physical evidence). The three last components are of special relevance for service companies.

Each set of these 7 P's are what we will call a Mix of Marketing, Marketing Mix, or MMIX. It is the combination of these 7 Ps that give rise to something unique, different and concrete. This concept is very important, since each MMIX will be directed towards a different customer segment, also unique. Therefore, everything that the company commercializes is materialized in those different MMIX.

Here is a quick example from the automobile industry. Each model is a MMIX that is aimed at a segment (target) selected among the multiple existing segments with its image, price and specific features. In the automobile business, the car type is even called the segment, the product, instead of the group of customers, due to the identification of the product with its market (the compact segment or the off-road segment).

Frequently, we tend to think that we can create a product and direct it to the entire market. "Why be self-limiting?" However, this does not work well; you have to create different products and market them in different ways to be able to approach the needs of clients of different types and with different needs or desires and be able to communicate well with each group. Managing an MMIX is not complicated but managing a lot at a onetime can be. Sometimes we will need to unify segments to facilitate this management.

This decision comes from the strategic phase. The tactical phase carries out the fine and detailed definition work of the 7 Ps. However, it is in the strategic phase that we define the segments, the targets, the type of product and the MMIX. We can begin to see how the details of the definition of the 7 Ps are tactical and easy to modify but the previous decisions that make them possible are much more important.

Tactics is built, then, on strategy. To develop the tactics you must first have the result provided by the strategy. Otherwise we will waste time and money. According to what we already know, the result of strategy is differentiation, the target to which it is applied and the positioning that the client perceives of all this.

The first P and perhaps the most important and intuitive is the product, where we will also include services. The product is easy to visualize and often it is the beginning or inspiration of our idea. Here in the tactical phase is where our design of the offering is going to take shape, where we will endow it with attributes. These attributes will be those perceived by the client but will build on a basis of differentiation previously established during the strategic phase. For example, a potential buyer of the Tesla model S will appreciate the attributes of the car reflected in its power, luxury and exclusivity, attributes that go on the basis of positioning an expensive car in the high segment, which is also electric. These attributes by themselves could have a much lower or nonexistent impact, as is the case of the Citroën C6 or the Nissan Leaf (sold in its segment), which occupy another spot on the customer positioning map.

All the actions to be taken in the tactics phase will reinforce the strategic design and will be developed from its foundation, always maintaining a coherent message aimed at the client.

It is interesting to identify that on many occasions the product 'per se' is something that has little intrinsic differentiation. We could call this the core product, the core or the base product. Let's take breakfast cereal as an example. There may be many different manufacturers that make very different products. But corn, wheat or oats are basically the same. These are the staples from which the rest of the products are made. Other components need to be developed for both the product and the service section. In accordance with the differentiation designed, the target and the position we want to obtain in the market, we will construct different types of augmented products.

An interesting case is what happened to the group formed by the brands Black & Decker, Walt and Stanley. The products that made up its portfolio were basically the same and of good quality. But the message sent to the market was confusing and as a result the different segments were not identified with the brands. The group had to create offering-target sets to reposition the brands in order to be perceived by the consumer market (B&D), the professional (deWalt) and the industrial (Stanley). This example may correspond, within the model of strategic drift, to when a bad tactic neutralizes a good strategy. A similar case occurred to SEAT, the car manufacturer a few years ago when an offer, perhaps too broad, with the complexity that this entails, along with too many similar models and without any saloon car confused users and damaged their business figures. Skoda, on the other hand, with only three models, had good results.

In addition to the increased product, families or product lines can be developed to better suit the needs of the different segments. In this way, the increased base product, enriched with services, is able to incorporate new differentiating components.

The other tool used to nurture differentiation is the business model. This is transmitted tactically through, people, the processes and to some extent channels (place) and physical evidence. It will be necessary to invest in employee development, training and encouragement in order to make them part of our project. Processes, on the other hand, have to be created. Sometimes you have to inspire or hire experts in certain fields of application. In others, we should lead ourselves by conceptualizing new processes that give rise to genuine business models. This part is very complicated and not very intuitive; it is perhaps the most difficult part of the entire marketing plan.

The remaining Ps have already been analysed previously, these are Price and Communication.

There are many books that talk about 7 Ps marketing, tactics. We have tried here to put it in perspective, explain that it must be sustained by a strong and concrete strategy and make a correspondence between its components and the sought after differentiation.

In summary, tactics are composed of coherent groups from the 7 Ps, called the MMIX, an MMIX for each offering / target. The offering is developed with the product, which encompasses the service, the increased product and the product lines and families. The business model is developed with the Ps of People, Place (channels), Processes and Physical Evidence. Finally we have the price and communication. Thus a specific differentiation is achieved for each MMIX.

13 THE SALES PROCESS

If the strategy of a company were good enough the sales process could be considered redundant. In its absence, the function of the commercial department of the companies must work much harder.

However, although our strategy was excellent, the design of sales processes must also be excellent and is an area for improvement to increase the competitiveness of companies. Designing a good sales function is not complicated; it requires comparison with the design of the strategy requirements and methodical execution.

In order to do this we can build on the work we have already developed. We have our customer base segmented on the one hand and our offering designed on the other. The first step is to select our customers in order to communicate our different offerings in the most efficient way.

Depending on the type of our clients, this could be done using online tools or by making in-person visits. In the first case, the sale has a greater communication component while the second is a more traditional component; in both cases we are visible to the customer, as we explained previously.

This process is obvious but what is not so obvious is the means of implementing it in a systematic manner; that is to say gradually covering all the territory in which our target customers are located, in the most efficient way for the company.

As a result of this activity, sales opportunities must be generated continuously. Some of these opportunities will be transformed into firm proposals and finally a percentage of them into sales. Therefore, many opportunities must be generated for us to obtain the appropriate percentage of sales. The sales process must establish a way to identify opportunities, communicate with the customer and follow this communication up, define the purchasing process (already studied in the segmentation process), establish the terms of the agreement and the closing conditions.

All of this does not have much science to it but requires methodology and discipline; this is one of the contributing factors as to why some companies penetrate more successfully in the markets than others. Selling is a fundamental activity that needs to be carefully designed, rigorously implemented, fostered in the company and remunerated through incentive schemes with shared benefits.

14 LEADERSHIP AND CHANGE

We have talked a lot about innovation, differentiation and materialization of an offering in a product and how to reach the customer through the strategy process. Obviously, all this does not happen spontaneously. It requires a lot of effort that deserves some reflection.

Working in the environment of strategy and innovation requires change and the management of that change. We all know the problems associated with Change Management, usually reflected in the form of immobility, internal resistance, weaknesses associated with previous systems and lack of acceptance of the new environment. Cultural changes are usually more difficult than technological changes. To achieve this, it is necessary to motivate the organization or group of people concerned; this is where leadership comes into play.

It is not easy to call collective action but when you know what you want, when you explain it well and when you see the objective "with your eyes", things become easier. That is why I place so much emphasis on customers seeing our strategy (positive perception) and on the company's employees clearly seeing the marketing plan, for example using SOSTAC®, or the strategic model, for example using MSSM®. When things are seen and understood, they "sell" better.

This means that the collaboration among members of the workforce increases as well as the contributions to the process. Let's recall that the innovation model of Nonaka and Takeuchi is largely based on communication and the discretionary contribution to the process.

That's why, when I talk about leadership I like to do it in the plural, Leadership with a capital "L", but also leadership with a small "l". We all have identified the Leader with a capital L, the person who in some exceptional and individual way is able to lead or guide others.

We do not usually identify very clearly the fact that the success of a leader depends on context and time. The leading person in the fifteenth century, captaining a ship across the Atlantic into the unknown might be a failure in our modern society and vice versa. I cannot imagine a great leader, for example, in the world of finance today triumphing in the middle ages.

Neither is the same style of leadership valid in all moments of life. Leadership among children tends to be based on physical abilities where a kind of physical bullying behaviour is often a resource, something that works badly in adulthood. I think of my childhood and I remember that most of the leading children were mediocre or unsuccessful adults, while many normal, shy or even weak children triumphed as they developed more emotional intelligence.

There are occasions and tasks that need hierarchical and authoritarian leaders and others, the current ones that require leaders known as "transformational", capable of managing change in complex organizations in a collaborative way. In this way, the concept of leadership is extended to leading organizations, leading teams, leading cities, leading societies.

In order to achieve this we have to count on the leaders with a small "l", the high-performance team members, those who work as part of a group or those ones who contribute quietly in the background, are vital to big organizations, large corporations and basically any team. Being a leader with a lowercase "l" is not always easy; you have to develop the culture. Large corporations obtain advantages, economies of scale in the markets, which small companies can never obtain.

Currently, messages that encourage the performance of an autonomous individual career based on personal innovation and leadership with a capital "L" are very fashionable. This is very good, but we also need to be educated to work as a team and contribute to the group with proud humility, knowing that the results of the group are usually better and more efficient. You have to be proud of belonging to the team that gets good results even if the visibility is carried by the forward players who score the goals or the cyclist who is "tête de la course."

In a globalized world, large organizations also have a great advantage in terms of knowledge management. **The cognitive act will always be done by people, but knowledge itself is in organizations**. To give an example, let's consider the company Airbus, the aircraft manufacturer. Quite possibly there is no one in the world who currently knows how to build a complete plane. If a certain worker leaves the company, the company will be able to replace them, but that worker, if he or she wants to continue building aircraft, must join another organization; sometimes taking with them their own team of professionals. To optimize knowledge management, it is necessary to foster a culture of collaboration and achieve reciprocal mutual trust and recognition between the company and the worker.

Moreover, a country without large enough organizations, capable of managing increasingly complex knowledge, will soon find its growth ceiling. A society that does not create large companies will become a society of industrial artisans, which is not necessarily bad, until you have to compete against the big multinationals. Then you lose. A balance is needed between the small, dynamic and resilient company and the large one, which has the financial capacity to undertake complex projects and **transmit complex knowledge** to another generation of workers.

Therefore, the Leader must know how to communicate and integrate the leaders (the members of their teams) in the common project. The basic traditional process of analyse – think – act, although valid, can be transmitted more smoothly with a model of visualize – feel – change (act) which is more empathetic and contributes towards developing team spirit. This can be done by performing the following actions:

- Recognizing problems
- Recognizing improvement capabilities
- Transmitting the vision
- Sensitive to needs and problems
- Motivating the different participants
- Acting, facilitating the process of change.

If this is done not only in the company but also throughout society, together with the participation of the government, we will have as a result a leading society. A society that does not care for its workers will hardly ever obtain their commitment. Societies that have achieved success in the past, such as Japan, Germany or even the United States, have offered a fulfilling career to their workers, including social benefits and retirement plans. The new schemes based on job insecurity are an experiment whose results we will observe in the coming decades.

Personal and corporate leadership for innovation

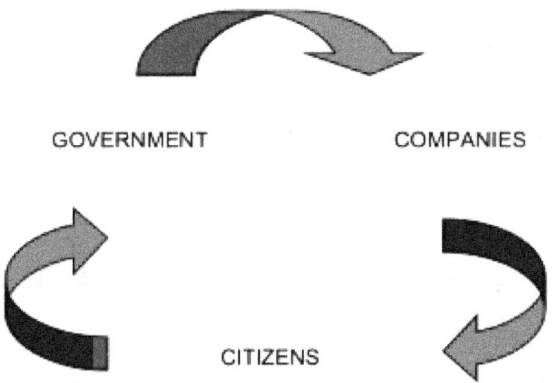

How can we trigger the process of change? A traditional method is benchmarking. Measuring yourself against others and improving processes simply by copying is also considered innovation. In fact, remember that one of the components of the Competitive Advantage was sustainability. If someone can easily copy what we have, we have no sustainable competitive advantage. So let's start by identifying what others do better than us and change, incorporating their best practices to match them. We can do this exercise at a human, social and also at a productive level.

At the same time, as we have seen, the organization must be prepared to incorporate the changes and improvements that are identified. This will not happen on its own. It is necessary to implement a process of innovation management in a systematic way where complex interdependencies will be identified that will have to be solved and where non-persecuted effects will arise; we need to be prepared in order to identify the unexpected.

To summarize:

1.- Benchmarking, what are others doing?

- At a social level, human
- A productive level, technological

2.- Prepare an organisation and its processes to:

- Implement an innovation management process systematically
- Solve complex interdependencies
- Identify effects not pursued

A business leader can encourage the participation and collaboration of its employees (leaders) with the following actions based on transformational leadership:

- Detecting the talent of its workers, encouraging their contributions to the company
- Sharing the vision, making it felt, creating a team, establishing common objectives and rewarding achievement

- Detecting signs of weakness early on, thinking and acting as a team
- Designing an innovation plan, monitoring and control, confronting reality
- Encouraging the generation of ideas
- Promoting active listening, the need to learn
- Assuming you have to fail often to achieve success first Consolidating the improvements achieved
- Surrounding yourself with volunteers, enthusiasts and experts
- Appreciating, sharing the credit and the project
- Believing in the process, sponsoring initiatives
- Creating cross-function, shared intelligence teams
- Remembering that attitude is contagious, set a good example
- Creating motivation for creative and innovative thinking
- Looking for anticipation, being proactive
- Maintaining an entrepreneurial attitude
- Stimulating versatile knowledge
- Stimulating creative dialogue
- Promoting diversity
- Boosting imagination

Obstacles to the process will arise. This is normal, it will always happen; you have to be prepared for it. There will always be resistance, scepticism, fear, doubt and uncertainty. You will have to try to identify this quickly and minimize it without falling into confrontation. We must maintain respect for everyone, based on generosity of spirit and absolute integrity.

Problems need to be spoken about and resolved. If this is not immediately possible, they should remain internal. If progress is difficult, it is preferable to abandon certain specific points. We must avoid, at all costs, the creation of groups and coalitions that lead to internal wars because once a toxic environment has been generated it is impossible to build an innovative collective.

On the other hand, a citizen, student, or employee, can develop their leadership qualities by working on the following areas:

- Search for personal productivity
- Strive, think what is best for everyone
- Be positive, think about contributing, no matter who benefits from it
- Find a fair work / family balance
- Try to implement a rational schedule
- Feeling proud of what you do well
- Recognising what we do wrong and changing it
- Proposing improvement processes

It is not only the Leaders who need to implement correct business strategy. Since strategy is a process that is distributed throughout the company and is also based on innovation, participation and internal communication, it will be necessary to create and stimulate the leaders with "l", (which should ideally include all employees, as is achieved in Japanese culture). This requires planning, effort and dedication. However, clear ideas and a solid frame of reference such as the one developed in this book will allow this communication to become more effective, clearly visualized and implemented more efficiently in the company.

Remember, use these tools and models to create and transmit your vision. Make the need for change felt and encourage the emergence of leaders to facilitate this process.

Naturally, all this must be based on mutual honesty and commitment. I am not going to ask for job security at this stage, but I will advocate commitment. A society in which politicians and companies exploit job insecurity, cannot build what is set out in this chapter. Within a system of young, underpaid employees or elderly workers expelled prematurely from the labour market, often forfeiting a large part of their pension, no leadership plan can succeed because there is no common project. The answer to this problem would need to be explored in another book. This change inexorably needs to be based on systems of mutual sharing and long-term success.

15 EPILOGUE

I hope that after reading this book you have been able to consolidate or place in order the multiple concepts and notions that are usually considered when we talk about strategy. My purpose in writing it is precisely to contemplate ideas in the form of a process and to achieve coherence between them.

By adopting a procedural point of view we can ensure that all the related components in the MSSM® model are valued and used. We will not neglect anything and we will not be tempted to depend on some happy go-lucky idea or an isolated strength.

Remember that in the long term success will come from the process of proper planning that contemplates and assimilates the changes that will inevitably occur in the environment. Therefore, the revision of the strategy will be continuous and this in turn implies the revision of all of its components. Even if unexpected good fortune comes your way occasionally, incorporate it into the process!

Explain your strategy. Create a discourse to be used within your company and also oriented towards your customers. Now you are in a position this discourse will be of sound content and will be properly articulated.

Do you recall that at the beginning of the book I asked you about your strategy? Maybe back then you had doubts; by now you should have the knowledge to be able to transmit your strategy clearly and directly, as well as identifying and proposing areas for improvement.

I truly hope that the content of this book has been useful to you and that you are successful in applying its ideas to your business.

MARKETING STRATEGY. CAN YOU TELL ME YOURS?

16 ABOUT THE AUTHOR

Hugo Rubio Vega is an Industrial Engineer, Master in Business Management, professional PgDip. in Marketing (Chartered Institute of Marketing, ACIM), MBA (Warwick Business School), Master in Philosophy, Science and Values and PhD in Philosophy, Science and Values. His professional career has been developed within the information technology industry and he has collaborated with university programmes.

https://www.linkedin.com/in/hugo-rubio-phd-1230401/

The process of business innovation gives rise to ideas that are consolidated into products and services. This process occurs continuously, in all workers, at all times and does not depend on work schedules. Therefore, every company must identify an innovation process, even if it is basic. Innovation is based more on well-managed intercommunication than on a technological department of Research and Development.

This is understood more comprehensively when framed within a business strategy model that is coherent, simple and manageable. With this purpose in mind this book introduces the Synthetic Model of Marketing Strategy MSSM® that guides the reader through the process of the creation and definition of a business strategy through the generation of ideas, ordering the concepts and leaving them all ready for incorporation into the company's marketing plan.

"Using this methodology we were able to redesign our offering to fit the market, increasing significantly our profit".

Begoña García. Programme Manager at Bilbao Formación. www.bilbaoformacion.com

"The MSSM® has been key to improving internal communication and optimizing our team's performance!.

Jose Fabián Pérez. Founder and Partner at Vitoria-Gasteiz Wine City Group. www.vitoriagasteizwinecity.es

"I realized we had to reposition our offering. Results improved along with brand image"

David de Bustos. Founder of Eventos Aizea. www.eventosaizea.com

"The methodology inspired me. I was able to generate and implement new and refreshing ideas"

Cristóbal Herrero. Partner at Demesel Metálicas. www.demeselmetalicas.com

"We shared the methodology with our clients, in order to improve communication and align objectives".

Roberto Alvarez. Partner at AdHoc Comunicaciones y Márketing. www.adhoc.es

www.ingramcontent.com/pod-product-compliance
Lightning Source LLC
Chambersburg PA
CBHW071414210526
45465CB00001B/385